Unexplained Places

UNEXPLAINED PLACES

EXPLORING MYSTERIES AROUND THE WORLD

Lee R. Schreiber

Illustrated
Books

A FRIEDMAN GROUP BOOK

BDD Illustrated Books
An imprint of BDD Promotional Book Company, Inc.
1540 Broadway
New York, N.Y. 10036

BDD Illustrated Books and the accompanying logo
are trademarks of the BDD Promotional Book Company, Inc.

99257

Copyright © 1993 by Michael Friedman Publishing
Group, Inc.

First Published in the United States of America in 1993
by BDD Illustrated Books.

ISBN 0 7924 5750 1

UNEXPLAINED PLACES
was prepared and produced by
Michael Friedman Publishing Group, Inc.
15 West 26th Street
New York, New York 10010

Editors: Kelly Matthews and Stephen Williams
Art Director: Jeff Batzli
Designer: Kevin Ullrich
Photography Editors: Christopher C. Bain and
    Grace How
Map Illustrations: Eugene M. Bak

Typeset by Trufont Typographers, Inc.
Color separations by United South Sea Graphic
    Arts Co.
Printed in Hong Kong and bound in China by Leefung-
    Asco Printers

Dedication

This one's for A, D, J, J, K, M & M for reasons which should not be a mystery.

Acknowledgments

Special thanks to Richard Amdur, Joyce Hackett, John Hanc, Kelly Matthews, and Stephen Williams for their invaluable contributions to this project.

Personally, I'm much obliged to Lisa Skriloff, Stan Kleckner, and Harv Zimmel.

CONTENTS

INTRODUCTION
8

NASCA
Writing on the Desert Floor
10

CARNAC
The Ancient French Stones
18

STONEHENGE
The Enigmatic Megalith on the
Salisbury Plain
26

ANGKOR WAT
Mysterious City in the
Cambodian Jungle
36

AYERS ROCK
Mystical Wonder of the Outback
46

MACHU PICCHU
City in the Sky
54

CERNE ABBAS
The Chalk Giant
64

GIZA
A Burial Site Fit for Kings
72

THE GREAT
SERPENT MOUND
The Prehistoric Native American
Earthwork
80

EASTER ISLAND
The Riddle of the South Pacific
90

GLASTONBURY
King Arthur's Reputed
Resting Place
98

PALENQUE
A Mayan Architectural Jewel
108

BIBLIOGRAPHY
118

INDEX
119

Introduction

Although there are thousands of extraordinary sites in the world, none are as historically rich, as topographically fascinating, and ultimately, as mysteriously mute as the twelve locations presented in this book.

Each unexplained place is described in great detail—the myths, the theories, the postulations—as well as any hard facts that have been unearthed. Everything that is known about each of these strange and baffling locations is revealed. Everything and nothing.

As we inch toward the twenty-first century, scientists are unraveling more and more of the many mysteries of our world. With state-of-the-art archaeological tools and techniques, little is left to the imagination; virtually all can be explained.

In some cases, however, new discoveries have only created additional questions. And what has become evident is that mere facts cannot unlock some eternal secrets.

As the reader wanders in and around these twelve special sites, wonder and awe will still be constant companions.

Some things (and places) just cannot be explained.

—L.R.S.

NASCA

Writings on the Desert Floor

Of the hundreds of lines, patterns, and figures indelibly etched onto two hundred square miles (517.8 sq km) of desert floor in southern Peru, some—such as the frog and spider (previous page)—are clearly recognizable to the aerial-based eye. Although they left few remnants of their civilization, the agrarian Nascas probably made pottery much like this male effigy figure (below), which scientists date some five hundred years after the Nasca period, around 1300 A.D.

© Evan Agostini, Private Collection

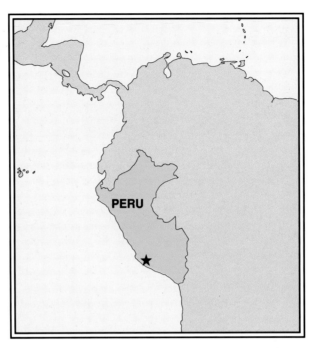

PERU

I t is the world's largest sketch pad, the most mammoth and extraordinary display of earthworks extant. Yet, the artists (no single artist could have worked on such a broad canvas) remain unknown, and there are no heirs to explain their creations.

What is the meaning of these drawings in the earth? Who drew them? How? When?

We now know half as much as we do *not* know about the two hundred square miles (517.8 sq km) of lines, patterns, and images etched onto the desert of southern Peru. For one, we do know when they were made—give or take a thousand years.

For those who eschew the landing-strip-for-extra-terrestrial-spaceships theory (although the gargantuan trapezoids, triangles, and rectangles do resemble runways and airports), these famous figures, lines, and designs were almost definitely created by the Nasca Indians between 500 B.C. and A.D. 500. Unfortunately, these impressive drawings are virtually the only remnants of the Nasca people to have survived the centuries. There are no contemporary Nascans, nor is there written history of their existence. Most of what we know about them is written on the desert floor in Peru.

The agrarian Nascas, who preceded the Incas, seemed to have been a playful people with an abiding love and respect for all living things. They were obviously very industrious as well: to reveal the yellow soil that serves as the "paint" for each of the hundreds of perfectly formed straight lines, intricate geometric patterns, and giant animal designs, the Nascas scraped away millions of rocks—by hand. (Thus far, there has been no evidence that they used or even had pack animals.) The precision of the lines as well as the accuracy of some of the anatomical renderings is amazing. For example, the reproduction of the 148-foot (45m) spider is apparently that of a rare species found only in the most remote portions of the Amazon. Visible on the spider's extended leg is the genus' unique reproductive organ. The amazing part is this: such a tiny feature can be seen only under a microscope. And as far as scientists and archaeologists can determine, there were no microscopes in Peru around the time of Jesus.

Joining the anatomically correct spider on the vast zoological landscape are a monkey, a snake, a llama, and a lizard that is more than 590 feet (179m) long. There are eighteen different birds (or bird shapes), ranging in length up to a very unbirdlike 902

© Steve Vidler/Leo De Wys Inc.

feet (274m). In terms of recognizable and detailed features, the most noteworthy are the giant condor (make that *giant*, giant condor) and the hummingbird, complete with outstretched wings and elongated food-seeking beak.

What makes these drawings even more amazing and unique is that they remained undiscovered by modern, aviation-oriented man until the 1920s. While there were vague references to giant lines and shapes made by Spanish explorers during the sixteenth and seventeenth centuries, Julio Tello—often called the *padre* of Peruvian archaeology—is credited with recording the Nasca drawings in 1926. For fifteen years afterward, the area remained relatively unnoticed—except for the enjoyment of passing airline passengers—until the arrival of an American archaeologist and professor of history, Dr. Paul Kosok.

On June 22, 1941—the day of the winter solstice in the southern half of the world—Kosok made a keen discovery. He observed that the setting sun met the horizon just above a straight line on which he was then standing. It was no coincidence, believed Kosok,

© Dave Bartruff/ FPG International

While many lines cross through the animal designs—leading scientists to theorize that the figures were rendered before the lines—other images seem to seamlessly intersect with lines, suggesting that they were created at the same time.

For her part, Reiche has documented and mapped hundreds of the Nasca lines and figures, while also being in the forefront of the fight to conserve and protect them. Reiche theorized that the lines helped predict the positions of the sun, moon, stars, and planets in order to help the Nascans plan their lives. Perhaps they could use the lines to determine the best time of year to plant and harvest crops, for example, as well as the time when the waters would swell the rivers.

In the late 1960s and early 1970s, however, scientists began debunking in earnest some of these beliefs. Using computer tests, they contended that the actual correspondences between the earthly lines and the stars above had about the same level of frequency as if they had been left to chance. In short, they believed that Kosok's revelation was indeed mere coincidence. American astronomer Gerald Hawkins, whose work at Stonehenge is widely respected (see page 31), was one of the ones who rejected the bulk of Reiche's theory. (For her part, Reiche charges that the statistical sampling used by Hawkins and others to gauge the accuracy of her work was not sufficient to be scientifically valid.)

but a clue to understanding that many of the seemingly random shapes and lines held a deeper, astronomically oriented significance.

Kosok called the Nasca area "the largest astronomy book in the world," a sentiment echoed by Dr. Maria Reiche, a respected German mathematician who studied the region for more than forty years. After Kosok's death in 1959, Reiche continued to advance the theories that Kosok had put forth on that winter's day in June.

"We will never know all the answers," Reiche has said, "and that is what a good mystery is all about."

Best-selling author Erich von Däniken, a proponent of the landing-strips-of-the-gods theory, suggested that extraterrestrial explorers visited southern Peru for a brief stay and then took off in their spaceships, leaving lines, or tracks, in the soil. According to von Däniken, the Nascans deepened these lines and then drew new ones in order to induce the otherworldly, presumably benevolent, astronauts to return. When that failed, they fabricated elaborate renderings of animals, insects, and birds—"sacrificial" symbols all.

One reason to eschew von Däniken's theory is strictly topographical. The soil in this part of the world is and was far too soft for large craft to land safely on it (presuming, of course, that the spaceships weighed more than, say, an Oxford dictionary).

Whether or not the Nasca Indians drew inspiration from extraterrestrials, it is likely that they created their magnificent designs on such a large scale in order to be viewed by gods dwelling in the heavens. But how were they able to construct such detailed and vast pictures—particularly since many of them were too big to be completely viewed from ground level?

Reiche suggested that the drawings were done by the Nasca people with the assistance of sophisticated surveying equipment "buried and hidden from the eyes of the [conquistadors] as the one treasure that was not to be surrendered." In the early 1980s, at least one archaeologist took a whack at this theory.

Joe Nickell of the University of Kentucky, who was doubtful that the Nascas possessed or needed any surveying skill or equipment, led a team of workers to a landfill in West Liberty, Kentucky. Using limited equipment—some rope, some stakes, and a wooden cross (to make right-angle measurements)—Nickell and his colleagues were able to replicate a 440-foot (134m) -long condor in the soil. They borrowed a concept introduced by Reiche—she had long stated that the Nasca used small mock-ups before attempting the larger-than-life-size creations—by preparing a scale drawing of the condor.

Nickell's group then marked off 165 points with stakes, attaching each of them with the twine. When a circular shape was needed, they used the stake-rope connection to inscribe it into the earth. All other curves were performed by hand. After finishing the great bird in the dark soil, they filled in the outline with powdered lime. The contemporary coup de grace was to photograph the "world's largest reproduction" from one thousand feet (304m) above the ground before it was entirely washed away by rain. (Considering the potential damage of rain, the continued presence of the Nasca drawings is an amazing phenomenon indeed. It also indicates how little rain has fallen in the Nasca Valley over the past ten thousand or so years.)

Nickell and company's findings provide some explanation as to how ancient people could perform earthly miracles with a rope and some stakes but still do not account for the almost mystical precision of the straight lines over such long distances. Many of the lines go on for miles; the longest is about forty miles (64km). In some instances, the lines deviate less than 6.5 feet (2m) over more than half a mile (0.8km).

There is a notion that the Nascans had some knowledge of flight, that their surveyors were able to fly through the skies in some type of ancient balloon. As improbable as that might seem, there is some corroboration to this theory. Thousands of pottery fragments were found throughout the Nasca Valley, and many of them feature what look like images of balloons and kites. Also, a number of circular "burn pits"—each of them containing blackened rocks—were discovered at the end of some lines. Could these have been possible launch sites for airborne ancients?

In 1975, Jim Spohrer, an American living in Peru, helped build a hot-air balloon from the materials and technology that he assumed would have been available to the ancient Nascas. Spohrer's *Condor I* was launched from an existing burn pit and reached a height of about 1,150 feet (350m) in its roughly three-mile (4.2km), twenty-minute flight. While certainly not conclusive, this experiment does lend credence to such fanciful theories.

The contemporary aerial photos of Nasca and its images are incredible and unforgettable, but the mysteries unearthed on and beneath the ground are equally revealing. A lot of what we do know about the Nasca people has been discovered in their graves. We know, for example, that they buried their dead in a fetal-like position, interring the deceased—along with some pottery and other artifacts—in prescribed burial grounds along the fertile walls of the valley. Archaeologists discovered one vast cemetery that had once held five thousand corpses; unfortunately, virtually all of them had been stripped bare by grave robbers over the years.

In addition to pottery fragments, countless stone piles similar to the totemic cairns found throughout Europe have been discovered in the Nasca Valley. Adjoining some of these groups of stones are remains of wooden posts, which may have been used to survey the land, thereby laying the groundwork for the huge patterns. There is also evidence of animal remains on the posts, indicating possible sacrifices.

Most scientists believe that many of the renderings of animals were drawn well before the lines. It's evident that the drawings were probably done in two separate stages, they say, because many of the lines cross over many of the animal designs. Some figures, however, would seem to have been drawn at the same time—like the great hummingbird, since its beak ends neatly on a (seemingly continuous) straight line.

Some have claimed that the long lines were really roads. However, since so many of these lines either end abruptly or lead on and on to nowhere, that is unlikely.

One compelling explanation that has recently emerged suggests that each line or pathway was a sort of family heirloom. That is, a specific family or a group of families were responsible for the upkeep of *their* line or lines. It was up to each kin-connected aggregation to maintain and preserve each line in their purview, keeping it free and clear of debris, vandalism, or other damaging effects. In some cases, an entire community could have been in charge of a line or a design. There is further speculation that the animal figures functioned as religious icons where the entire group would congregate to worship or perhaps to give thanks on a specific Nascan "holiday."

The Nasca Valley remains an unexplained place because we don't know for certain why there were so many lines and figures drawn, nor even why the figures were so big and the lines so straight. What we still don't know about Nasca could fill up a sketchbook.

A very, very large one.

Although only fragments of pottery have been unearthed in Nascan gravesites, these fragments, if reconstructed, would likely resemble this ceramic vase with its agricultural motif.

The Aymara

paths, have been worn through over the centuries in rituals that honor the natives' ancestors. Many of these lines ascend hillsides, on whose summits the spirits of ancestors are believed to dwell, and culminate in shrines that invariably face east. On certain festival days, before heading up the paths to these shrines, the Aymara will stop at intervals to make sacrifices of small animals.

Again, the Nasca lines could be seen as pathways to heretofore undiscovered lands, and the drawings could be interpreted as offerings to gods or ancestors. Unfortunately—or fortunately for those who prefer their history laden with mystery—the Nasca figures remain in the realm of much theory and little fact.

Lake Titicaca, the world's highest navigable lake (below), is home to the Aymara Indians, whose earth lines are similar to those drawn by the Nasca perhaps two thousand years before. On Taquile Island (left), an Aymara man knits while his wife spins wool.

THE NASCA AREA, NEAR THE PACIFIC OCEAN ON THE west coast of Peru, lies roughly equidistant from three other major Peruvian venues—Lima, the capital city; the ruins of Machu Picchu, the lost Inca city (see page 54); and Lake Titicaca, the world's highest navigable lake. While there are no Nascan descendants to help explicate some of the mysteries of the earth drawings, the Aymara Indians—who still reside near Lake Titicaca and can date their ancestry back to the sixteenth century B.C.—can provide clues to their own blood- and earth lines.

In and around the villages of the Aymara are straight lines similar to those of the Nasca region. These lines, or

CARNAC

The Ancient French Stones

On the southwestern coast of Brittany, France, the great and small megaliths at Carnac (previous page) predate the standing stones of Stonehenge by more than two thousand years.

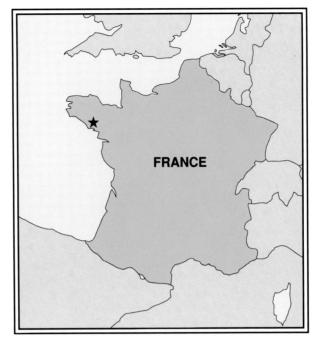

FRANCE

The megaliths in and around Carnac—located on the southwest coast of Brittany in France—are the oldest monuments in Europe, predating Stonehenge in England by more than two thousand years. And while the English edifice stands as a unique construction—perhaps the most renowned on earth—it is dwarfed by the sheer magnitude of these ancient French stones.

In number, size, and weight, there is certainly no contest. Stonehenge has eighty stones and Carnac has four thousand, and while the heaviest rock on the famed British monument weighs about fifty tons (46t), Le Grand Menhir Brisé (often called the "Fairy Stone") found on French soil is the largest stone ever quarried and moved in ancient Europe. Before shattering into four clean chunks—it was believed to have fallen during an earthquake in 1722—the great pillar measured sixty-five feet (19.8m) high and weighed more than 350 tons (319t).

This is *the* megalith ("great stone") of all European megaliths. Recent scientific surveys theorize that it was a "focal point for studying the movements of the moon," although most still believe that because of its presence near a burial mound, its true significance was to "guard" the dead. On its own, the huge Fairy

Stone remains only a relatively small piece in the entire puzzle of Carnac.

"[Carnac] is one of archaeology's most enduring mysteries," says Evan Hadingham, a British author who has visited and studied Stonehenge as well. "It poses as many tantalizing unanswered questions as the pyramids." After at least two hundred years of scientific scrutiny, Carnac's secret code remains, for the most part, unbroken.

One of the key questions, however, was answered recently. For centuries, historians were convinced that these megaliths were built by the Gauls, Celtic people living in France, for their priests, the Druids. Although there was speculation as early as the mid-eighteenth century that the great stones of Carnac might be pre-Celtic, it wasn't until 1959 that scientists—using radiocarbon dating techniques—finally came up with a relatively finite, if seemingly impossible, date of approximately 4300 B.C. The oldest date they were able to assess in the area was 4650 B.C. for the establishment of the gloomy passage grave of Kercado, which is near Carnac.

To use a stone or set of stones as a sacred memorial or relic is obviously a universal trait. Evidence of this is found in every corner of the earth. Few ancient cultures, however, were as industrious in erecting these memorials as those of western Europe, and nowhere were the locals more diligent and enthusiastic in constructing what have proven to be age-old monuments than at Carnac. The picturesque French countryside is simply awash in menhirs, cromlechs, and dolmens (see page 22).

More than fifty dolmens—with chambers of varying sizes and shapes—dot the landscape of Carnac and its environs. The surrounding woods and moors are littered with hundreds of solitary menhirs, up to thirty-one feet (9.4m) in height. But the most extraordinary and memorable view is that of the alignments of menhirs—forests of stone slabs—that stretch on row after row. It is a breathtaking sight, almost too vast to take in at once.

A French antiquary, the Chevalier de Freminville, took a good, long look at these megalithic avenues in 1827, and certainly his description is still apt today: "The numbers of these stones in bizarre arrangements,

the height reached by their long, grey, mossy outlines rising from the black heather in which they are rooted, and finally the total stillness that surrounds them, all astound the imagination and fill the soul with a melancholy veneration for these ancient witnesses to so many centuries."

Standing in "total stillness," four different alignments of avenues reach for almost five miles (8km) through forests and farmlands, beginning in the small town of Le Menec just north of Carnac. The first alignment, 1,099 menhirs arranged side by side in descending height on eleven separate avenues, extends eastward from a group of old stone cottages in Le Menec. The stones adjoining the cottages—those that are still standing—stand up to 13 feet (4m) in height, while the ones at the end of this alignment are only about three feet (0.9m) high. The stones are spaced irregularly, and the rows curve gently toward the northeast for about two-thirds of a mile (1.1km) before ending at a stand of pinewoods.

© Fridmar Damm/Leo De Wys Inc

Approximately four thousand stones punctuate the picturesque French countryside in and around Carnac.

Megalithic Meanings

MEGALITHIC CONSTRUCTIONS COME IN SEVERAL FORMS.

Menhirs—big, tall pillars jutting out of the earth; the word is from the Breton (a Celtic dialect), meaning "long stones." The largest freestanding menhir, the Kerloaz menhir in Finistere in westernmost Brittany, is forty feet (12.2m) from top to bottom.

Cromlechs—clusters of menhirs in circular formations (Stonehenge being the most famous); the word is from the Breton for "curved stones."

Dolmens—the most popular form of megalithic monuments found in Europe (again, from the Breton); in essence, they're ancient tombs in the form of chambers constructed through various kinds of stone formations.

The many manifestations of megaliths (clockwise from left): a menhir, *or long stone; the most* famous cromlech, *or circular cluster of menhirs, at Stonehenge; an* alignment, *or rows after rows of clustered menhirs; a* dolmen, *or ancient tomb.*

All dolmens are built, at least in part, with a minimum of two vertical stones capped by a large slab; larger dolmens may have dozens of side stones with a row of massive capstones for the roof. Most dolmens are buried beneath a mound of soil to form a chamber that is usually round or oblong, although square or polygonal ones have occasionally been found. The largest one is likely the Bagneux dolmen in western France, which is constructed of nine sidepieces and four capstones; it measures sixty-one feet (18.5m) in length. The capstones themselves are all at least two feet (61cm) thick, and the largest of them weighs eighty-six tons (78t). It's been calculated that about three thousand men would have been needed to set this dolmen in place.

When menhirs are organized in row after row, the resulting construction is called an *alignment*.

To the east, over a rise, is the next set of alignments at Kermario ("place of the dead"). Although there are only seven rows, the menhirs here are appreciably larger and stretch even farther than those of Le Menec. These range up to twenty-three feet (7m) in height, and they, too, diminish in size as they extend to the east. This alignment extends about three-quarters of a mile (1.2km).

Another narrow forest intrudes before the Kerlescan ("the place of the burning") alignments commence. These thirteen parallel rows, which extend for a comparatively scant four hundred yards (365m) and consist of 540 stones, seem to end abruptly—at the town of Kerlescan itself. The last, and smallest, alignment, which consists of one hundred stones, begins and ends at Le Petit Menec.

Curiously, even though these stones are a throwback to antiquity, there seems to have been no written record of them until the eighteenth century. That lack, of course, did nothing to slow the parade of tall tales and mythical lore that served as gospel until some science could be introduced.

At the head of this fanciful parade was the legend of Cornely, patron saint of Carnac and cattle (and a former Pope). The story goes that as he was fleeing the legions of Rome, he headed for his native Brittany, bringing with him only a pair of oxen to carry his belongings. Climbing a hill north of what is now Carnac and seemingly trapped by Roman soldiers, he effected a lifesaving miracle: he turned the pursuing warriors to stone. And so, the rows of granite markers are actually Roman soldiers—each different from the next—petrified for eternity.

While most eighteenth-century intellectuals rejected this explanation for the megaliths of Carnac, virtually

all believed—and many scientists continued to believe up until the carbon dating in 1959—that the great menhirs were from the great Caesar's day. They further speculated that the alignments were Druid artifacts.

Other theories ranged from the mundane (the rows of menhirs were erected by the Romans as windbreaks for their tents) to the profane (routes along which men could find prostitutes), not to mention the sporting (markers for ancient forms of cricket or golf) as well as the obligatory extraterrestrial explanation (another landing strip for spaceships).

Up until recently—as with the giant of Cerne Abbas across the Channel (see page 64)—the megaliths of Brittany have been used as part of ancient fertility rituals. At Cruz-Moquen, women raise their skirts to the dolmen, aiming to become pregnant. And in another May Day evening ritual, childless women would slide bare-bottomed along the prone stones of Le Grand Menhir Brisé.

Also, there is sufficient scientific authority to argue that the dolmens and menhirs were used—as some have said of Stonehenge—to chart and measure the suns, stars, and moons.

While this theory was more or less broached in the latter nineteenth century, the most authoritative argument advancing the astronomical purpose of the megaliths was made in the mid-1970s by Alexander Thom, a retired professor of engineering from Oxford. The then-eightyish Thom energetically crisscrossed and charted the countryside around Carnac, figuratively turning over every stone to bolster his findings. At the conclusion of his work, he contended that, in essence, the megaliths were a form of sophisticated lunar laboratory.

The keystone to his research was Le Grand Menhir Brisé. Using the Fairy Stone as a sighting device—to mark reference points along the horizon—Thom claimed that moonrises and moonsets could be observed. Eclipses could even be predicted.

Subsequent scientists, including Evan Hadingham, have carefully examined Thom's lunar thesis. And while Hadingham agrees that Thom's work legitimized the possibility of "megalithic astronomy," he believes that "it is a mistake to visualize Neolithic people as high-tech scientists. The most convincing alignments to the sun and moon are clearly not remnants of a research program, but part of a complex set of religious ideas—many of which we'll never know."

What do we know? For certain, not much. But, according to most scholars, we can make several educated guesses. If there are less than three thousand stones still standing, there probably were upward of ten thousand at one time. As for the meaning of the megaliths themselves, the isolated menhirs were most likely used as topographic markers, commemorative stones, and/or fertility icons. The alignments could have been used for processionals, perhaps for herding cattle. In addition to functioning as burial tombs, the dolmens could indeed have helped chart planets (most of them face the sun exactly at the point it rises on the summer solstice; and the alignments clearly move from west to east).

Trying to crack the case of the Carnac avenues without a written road map is not easy; thousands of years of mystery lie buried beneath these silent markers. But the fun is in exploring and sifting through the clues. The stones of Carnac, however, may never reveal anything more definitive than truly great and serene beauty.

After centuries of speculation concerning Carnac's megalithic origins, scientists—using radiocarbon dating—finally pinned down an approximate date of 4300 B.C.

STONEHENGE

The Enigmatic Megalith on the Salisbury Plain

Scientists are still trying to shed some light on the creation and function of the magnificent architectural feat we know as Stonehenge (previous page).

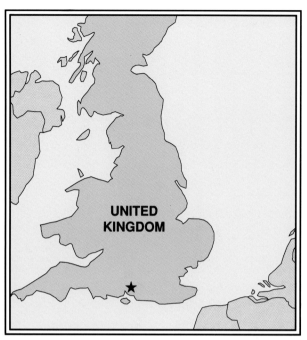

UNITED KINGDOM

Head north from the small British town of Salisbury, out into the open plains where chalky soil encourages the growth of deep green grass. The land is flat, the earth itself pitted and uneven. On the horizon, the rocks of Stonehenge stand in sharp relief, rising out of this dramatic landscape like dark giants caught in a strange circle dance. Hummocks and furrows—the fingerprints of man's past, the evidence that this was a place where civilization was born—scar the ground that must be crossed to reach this startling monument.

Many such cromlech sites exist throughout the British Isles, but Stonehenge remains the most famous and enigmatic of them all. Its remote location and complex design have invited centuries of casual, as well as scientific, speculation. Most who have gazed upon it have found Stonehenge as haunting and wondrous as any site on earth. Cloaked in myth and legend, shrouded in conjecture, the creation and function of this prehistoric architectural feat is an ongoing subject of study for archaeologists and other experts. Perhaps the best way to shed a little light on the mystery of Stonehenge is to examine the forms it has taken over the millennia and the people who may have created it.

Stonehenge, named by the Saxons, who also called it the "hanging stones," was built over a period of nearly five hundred years, during which time three major cultural shifts occurred. Amazingly, the basic design of the structure was kept the same, as were its original alignments.

Originally, Stonehenge had been built by the local Neolithic agrarian community as little more than an imposing earthwork. A huge circular ditch was carved out of the land, leaving an earthen bank that archaeologists have since calculated was at least six feet (1.8m) high and equally wide, with a diameter of 320 feet (97m). At the center of the construction stood a building, perhaps measuring up to 100 feet (30m) across, of which only the postholes remain. Even at its inception, the alignment of Stonehenge was of great importance; the entrance to this assemblage was oriented directly southward. The Heel stone, or Helestone, as it is also known, marks the entrance to Stonehenge on the southern avenue. It is over this stone that the sun rises during the midsummer solstice, an event that continues to attract thousands of onlookers.

It was an invasion of the so-called Megalith Builders, who overran Britain from the European mainland, that apparently brought new ideas to the building of Stonehenge. During this period, from 2000 to 1700 B.C., a ring of fifty-six craters—dubbed the "Aubrey holes" after John Aubrey, the antiquarian who discovered them in the seventeenth century—was added to the earthwork. Also during this period, bluestones were incorporated into the concentric plan to form two rings, one closed and the other open-ended. These bluestones were extremely difficult to obtain; their source was not discovered until 1923, when the British geologist H. H. Thomas found the small area where they had been quarried in the Welsh Prescelly Mountains. Eighty of these precious stones had somehow been transported almost 300 miles (483km) over land and across water to adorn the Stonehenge site. Scien-

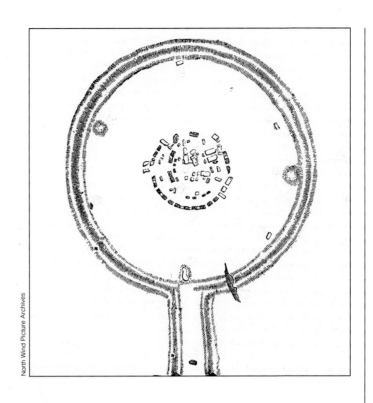

North Wind Picture Archives

© Nancy S. Diturl/Envision

Although Stonehenge (left) was built over a period of five hundred years, the basic design and structure was maintained—as evinced by its current ground plan (above left).

North Wind Picture Archives

While scientists and artists have long attempted to envision Stonehenge's original glory (above and opposite), there is perhaps something even more powerful and beautiful about its present-day state.

tists speculate that the stones were floated around the Welsh coast by raft, then pulled arduously overland on crude sleds.

The changes in Stonehenge were also concurrent with the emergence of a new culture in the area, characterized by the pottery excavated at the site. Known as the "Beaker People" for the shape of the vessels they used, they were thought by some experts to have been primarily sun worshipers. They were also credited with having engineered a minor but distinct shift of Stonehenge's center to align it more exactly with the Heel stone and the rising sun of the midsummer solstice. The Beaker People also constructed a two-mile (3.22km) earthen bank, which formed an avenue extending to the banks of the River Avon.

Undoubtedly the greatest additions to Stonehenge were made by the Wessex people around 1500 B.C. at

the height of the Bronze Age. By uprooting the rows of bluestones, they cleared the way for the mammoth Sarsen blocks that have come to characterize Stonehenge. These twenty-one-foot (6.4m) blocks of sandstone, some weighing as much as fifty tons (45t), were transported from the downs at Wiltshire, an excruciating twenty-mile (32km) trip that included negotiating a steep slope. We may never know why these particular blocks of stone were considered so indispensable—not to mention how they were actually cut. Indeed, the stones were dressed with great accuracy, utilizing a mortise-and-tenon, or ball-and-socket, construction that lent permanence to the post-and-lintel design. Equally startling from a design aspect is the fact that Stonehenge rests on a slightly sloping plain from west to east, yet the lintel stones are *even*; this no doubt required very precise calculations and great skill that seem unusually advanced for these ancient builders.

The archways, or trilithons as they are called because of their triple stone arrangement, form the main circle, or cromlech (see page 22), and horseshoe patterns still visible today, while the bluestones were rebuilt in an interior ring and arc around the flat green sandstone centerpiece known as the Altar stone.

A final mystery concerning the Sarsen stones is how the builders knew to employ *entasis*, a sophisticated technique used to reduce optical distortion by adjusting the proportions of the rocks. There has been conjecture that this knowledge was somehow carried to Stonehenge from the Mediterranean: the Mycenaean and Minoan civilizations of Greece and Crete employed entasis regularly in their architecture. But this theory seems questionable, since work on Stonehenge had virtually ended by the time the Mediterranean cultures were in their ascendancy. Regardless of how and where their ideas were generated, the creators of Stonehenge were without a doubt masters of their art. The lasting nature of the construction stands as a testament to their genius and diligence. But to what end? What purpose did this incredible feat of engineering serve?

One of the most reasonable answers to the question of Stonehenge's function is proffered by Gerald S. Hawkins, the British astronomer, or "astro-archaeologist," as he is also known. In 1963, after many years of study and experimentation, he became convinced that the structure was built as a kind of stone-age computer to chart aspects of the heavens and predict celestial events. While other scientists have discounted some of Hawkins' theories, claiming that there is little accuracy afforded by the structure when mapping the course of stars, few dispute his findings that Stonehenge is a quite serviceable lunar and solar calendar (which also lead many to believe that Stonehenge was a religious complex). The specificity of some twenty-four alignments with the Heel stone, Altar stone, archways, and other features of the site underscore the validity of these opinions.

Hawkins also discovered that the Aubrey holes on the perimeter of the area could be used to forecast lunar eclipses if six stones were inserted in a certain order, then moved around the circle one hole a year. This is the most intriguing idea to have been postulated concerning the use of the Aubrey holes. Other notions include their use as offering pits into which sacramental liquids were poured and as symbolic passageways to the "otherworld."

The latter thought is not so farfetched considering that the Aubrey holes were indeed used as burial places for cremated human remains, but only long

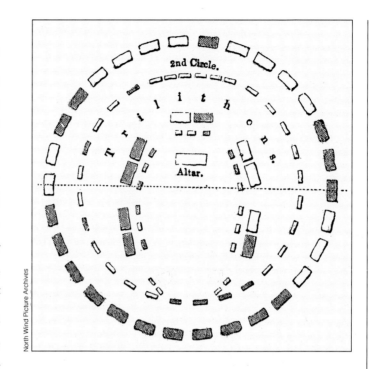

after they were originally dug. In fact, the remains found at Stonehenge point to the possibility that from the very beginning, the central wooden building in the first phase of construction served as a kind of mortuary. Some weight has been given to the theory that the early site may have hosted ceremonies in which ancestral remains were ritually exposed to the sun.

The allegation that Stonehenge was built by and for the Druid priests, heretofore the best-known hypothesis, is probably the only one that has decisively been rejected as false. The Druids, a cult that presided over the pagan Celts of the British Isles (and Gaul), were associated with Stonehenge through the writings of John Aubrey, an association later echoed by William Stukeley, an eighteenth-century antiquarian. It was only with the advent of radiocarbon dating in the mid-1960s that their theories were disproved. Colin Renfrew, the British archaeologist responsible for the breakthrough studies, found that Stonehenge actually predated the Druids by more than one thousand years. It is certainly conceivable, however, that the Druids adopted the mystical site as a place of worship later on, tailoring the awesome components to suit their sacrificial needs.

Through the centuries many tales have circulated regarding the genesis of this endlessly fascinating place. Unlikely participants in the birth of Stonehenge have included such famous characters as Merlin the magician and even Satan himself, who was rumored to have created it simply to stump the best efforts of mankind to figure it out. Other legends were propagated by various peoples who adopted the already ancient Stonehenge as their own—such as the Romans, who left offerings of pottery and coins, and many centuries later, the Normans, who sang the praises of Britain's illustrious past by incorporating Arthurian legends into the creation of Stonehenge. It was the Normans who passed down the first surviving written reference to the great ring of rocks to modern archaeologists. The Angles, the Saxons, and the Jutes, it may be assumed, all stood in awe of Stonehenge, applying their own ideas of the world to its formation and interpreting its mysteries in the way they knew best.

More contemporary investigators have taken a less conventional path in the evolution of their theories about Stonehenge. One of the more provocative of these researchers is T.C. Lethbridge, an archaeologist who also explores psychic events. He believes that the construction and alignments of Stonehenge created a powerful energy force field that was transmitted across the land to encourage the growth and good health of crops and people. Although this energy network fell into disuse centuries ago, unexplained phenomena, including electrical shocks suffered by experimenters

and photographs that displayed unusual emanations of light from the Sarsen stones, have since been recorded at Stonehenge. Many theories have arisen that the structure was somehow used in magical ceremonies based on the engraved markings that cover many of the trilithons. These carvings, frequently in the form of a cup-and-rings pattern, were laid out with a mathematical precision that belies any thought that their purpose was merely decorative. The question remains as to why these prehistoric builders chose a cromlech design in the first place, since the mammoth proportions of Stonehenge prevent a true appreciation of the design unless viewed from the air. The arrangement of the stones is hardly a fluke. More than nine hundred clusters of standing monoliths have been found in England, Scotland, and Wales, but none are as imposing as Stonehenge.

While the true secrets of this mystical place have yet to be uncovered, the standing stones are a reminder that technology is a poor substitute for wisdom: although the wheel was not yet in use, our ancestors still managed to construct a prehistoric "mini— Mount Palomar"—a relatively accurate astronomical gauge.

Although its age-old appeal has been constant, conjecture concerning Stonehenge ranges from the prosaic to the supernatural. For thousands of years, it has drawn curious observers from all over the world. To this day, Stonehenge hosts members of the ancient Druidic order who still celebrate the midsummer solstice on its sacred ground. For the countless others who make the journey to the great Salisbury plain merely to gaze upon it, Stonehenge is a monument to the unknown, an ancient place that is far greater than the sum of its awe-inspiring parts.

Who Goes There?

CONSIDER, FOR A MOMENT, THE MEN WHO BUILT STONE-henge: attired in animal skins or crude flaxen cloth, these prehistoric humans, our ancestors, hunted for their meat, preying on bison, deer, and wild boar. The game they hunted represented primal strength and endurance; there was little room in their culture for feebleness. The growing of crops was limited, and ornaments for the hair and body were designed from metal and bone. These men and women had no use for furniture; life in their huts was conducted squatting on the beaten clay or dung floors. How could these people, who never even recorded the history of their hunts with paint—as did their more ancient cousins at Altamira—be responsible for designing and building the advanced celestial observatory known as Stonehenge?

It is not difficult to understand why John Aubrey, the grandfather of modern Stonehenge studies, believed that the site at Salisbury could only be the work of the powerful and mysterious Druids. Although it has been proven time and again that these Celtic priests came to the British Isles one thousand years after the creation of Stonehenge, the misconception remains to this day, giving the sect a kind of theoretical preeminence. Why should this be so?

Some scientists believe that a site as mysterious and perplexing as Stonehenge (right) could only have been built by a sect as shadowy and complex as the Druids. Depicted in the illustration opposite, a Druidic human sacrifice is threatened by the arresting Romans.

The Druids' reputation seems as mysterious and per-plexing as that of Stonehenge. No written history of their rituals and practices has survived, if there ever was one. So little is known about the Druids that they, like their holy place, live mainly in the realm of speculation. They remain, to this day, a shadowy and complex hierarchy of princely intellectuals.

Archaeologist Gerald S. Hawkins points out that con-temporary local guides to Stonehenge will still thrill their visiting charges with tales of the deeply grooved chan-nels where "the warm blood of Druid victims ran." Hawkins notes also that the Roman emperor Caesar men-tioned Stonehenge in a book called *Gallic Wars*, describ-ing a practice attributed to the Druids during a harvest festival wherein "figures of immense size, whose limbs, woven out of twigs, they fill with living men and set on fire, and the men perish in a sheet of flame." There is in-deed a long history of human sacrifice connected to the agricultural development of early man, but this, too, has earlier roots than the Druids.

Another ritual linked with Celtic worship that proba-bly predates the Druids was the Beltane Fire. All across the British Isles, fires were ignited on specific celestial calendar days such as the spring and fall equinoxes, mid-summer's eve, and midwinter. Usually lighted in twos, these fires acted as gateways for men and animals to pass through, perhaps for spiritual purification. Beltane Fires were assumed to be representative of the Druidic sun god, but one can only guess as to the variety of symbolic meanings the fires may have had in the days before the Celts.

Stonehenge continues to attract the followers of this cryptic cult. Dressed in white robes and hoods, modern-day Druids provide an eerie spectacle—one that may conjure images of pre-Celtic gatherings with their skin cloaks and painted faces. The numbers of Druidic visi-tors are fewer now since the British authorities have cur-tailed visits for fear of grave damage to the rocky marvel. So many people have trod the chalky paths that the site

North Wind Picture Archives

is in danger of being irreparably damaged, and during busy holidays, police cordons and rolls of barbed wire protect the portals of Stonehenge.

There has even been talk of creating a counterfeit Stonehenge, molded from fiberglass or Styrofoam, that could receive hands-on attention while sparing the real thing from wear and tear. Naturally this idea has gener-ated more laughter than funding. But who knows? There may yet be a Foamhenge in our future.

ANGKOR WAT

Mysterious City in the Cambodian Jungle

Covering an area of one square mile (2.6 sq km), the world's largest stone monument, Angkor Wat (previous page), was constructed without mortar and dedicated to the Hindu god Vishnu.

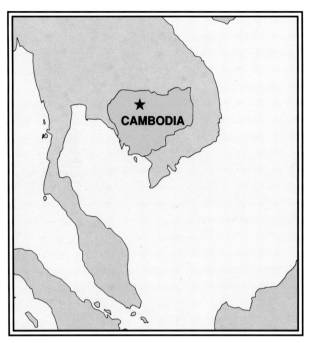

Built without mortar in the tropical jungle of northwestern Cambodia, the temple of Angkor Wat has remained one of the greatest architectural triumphs of all time. The twelfth-century masterpiece, which covers an area of one square mile (2.6 sq km), is also a great architectural mystery.

We know, for example, that the Khmers built Angkor Wat, but we don't know why the world's largest stone monument has so many similarities to the eighth-century Mayan pyramids at Palenque (see page 108), which were constructed four hundred years earlier more than halfway around the world. Were the Mayan and Khmer cultures both derived from one ancient culture? And what precipitated the fall of the great Khmer empire? Was Angkor Wat designed and arranged as (another) ancient observatory? Perhaps the biggest mystery of all is how this magnificent structure has managed to withstand centuries of warring political factions and the encroachment of nature.

Around A.D. 1000, sprawling, multicultural Angkor was reputed to have been the world's largest city. Originally covering thirty-eight square miles (99 sq km), Angkor was filled with temples, shrines, reservoirs, and irrigation canals and had an estimated population of five hundred thousand (some say it may have reached one million during the late twelfth century).

For much of the period between the ninth and the fifteenth centuries, Angkor was the capital of the ancient Khmer empire—one of the largest empires in the history of Southeast Asia—encompassing all of present-day Cambodia and much of Vietnam, Laos, and Thailand.

The Khmers' most prevalent system of political and religious beliefs was Indian in origin, and their religion was a form of Hinduism. Angkor Wat was dedicated to the Hindu god Vishnu.

Angkor's first great king was Jayavarman II, who purportedly liberated his people from Japanese domination in the ninth century and at the same time introduced an ancient Indian royal cult into the Khmer realm. This cult elevated each secular ruler to semisacred status by spiritually associating him with one of several Hindu gods. Each king was supposed to build a large stone temple, or temple-mountain, that would become his tomb upon his death. It was believed that the dead king then merged into the god with whom he had been associated in life, and the tomb subsequently became the symbolic home of the god-king.

© Alan Hinerfeld

More than seventy temples in Angkor testify to the success of this cult, with a royal edifice complex that covered an area more than three times the size of Manhattan. Hundreds of architects and engineers and thousands of laborers worked years at a time to create these masterpieces of religious art.

Jayavarman II worshiped Shiva, and it was this god's creative energy that was to inhabit the king's lifeless body after he departed his earthly realm. Certainly the monarch did not go precipitously into that good night; he reigned for sixty years.

During his tenure, Jayavarman II literally changed the face of his country; he also changed its name—from Chenla to Kambuja (forerunner of Cambodia's modern-day name, Kampuchea). No subsequent Khmer king ruled Kambuja for as long, but many of Jayavarman's successors left an indelible imprint on their people and their land.

Indravarman I, who ruled from A.D. 877 to 889, initiated sophisticated irrigation techniques that not only increased the rice harvests but also increased the region's urban population. The ancient kings believed

Built by King Suryavarman II in the twelfth century, Angkor Wat ("temple of the capital") served as a temple during the king's lifetime and then as a tomb after his death.

The Monuments of Jayavarman VII

King Jayavarman VII, the last of the great Khmer rulers, dedicated two great temples to his mother and father, then built the Bayon (right), the largest and most elaborate monument of them all, for himself. Plain, simple Preah Khan (far right)—built just north of Angkor Thom in homage to Jayavarman's father— has, for the most part, withstood the ravages of man and nature.

KING JAYAVARMAN VII (A.D. 1181–1220) WAS THE LAST of the great Khmer rulers. After his demise, the Kambujan empire began a steady decline, which probably reached its nadir with the Thai conquest in the fifteenth century. During his lifetime, however, the people of Angkor thrived—its population may even have reached one million—as did its architectural development. Jayavarman's three most memorable achievements include the jungle monuments of Ta Prohm, Preah Khan, and the Bayon—which were built for his mother, his father, and himself, respectively. All three shrines are located within or near the walled city of Angkor Thom, which was Jayavarman's capital.

The Ta Prohm temple, which lies outside the city to the east, is probably in the most disheveled condition. Tangled vines and moss cover much of the outer walls, threatening its very structure. When a French team of conservators worked on the monument in the early part of the twentieth century, they chose not to clear away most of the growth; to do so, they contended, would have required dismantling it.

Even though the Ta Prohm temple is dedicated to the king's mother, the sandstone entranceway features four stone smiling faces all representing her son, Jayavarman.

Located just north of Angkor Thom and covering nearly one-half of a square mile (1.3 sq km), the monument built to honor the king's father is in fairly decent shape. The French archaeologists apparently devoted more time to its restoration than they did on Ta Prohm before being expelled from the country. Also, few recent visitors have been allowed in this shrine.

Inside and out, Preah Khan is plainer and simpler, although the motifs in the shrine have the same combina-tion of Hindu and Buddhist images that are found at the other two temples of Jayavarman VII.

As for the Bayon, the king's own monument, it is located precisely in the center of Angkor Thom. From above, the shrine's towers and galleries can be seen to form a mandala, a concentric design that symbolizes the universe. On many of the walls throughout the Bayon, sculptural reliefs celebrate the victorious battles of the

Khmer ruler. On the outside are fifty-four huge towers, each one intricately sculptured with Jayavarman's Buddha-like likeness. While most of the previous Khmer rulers embodied Hindu gods, Jayavarman VII was said to be the living incarnation of the great Buddha.

On his visit to the Bayon around the turn of the century, the French travel writer Pierre Loti described his unease with the king's excess: "I shudder suddenly with an indefinable fear as I perceive, falling upon me from above, a huge, fixed smile; and then three, and then five, and then ten. They appear everywhere, and I realize that I have been overlooked from all sides by the faces of the quadruple-visaged towers."

© E.F. Anderson/Visuals Unlimited

that whoever controlled the water controlled the land, so the Khmers developed a system of irrigation using canals, dikes, moats, and large reservoirs that was much more advanced than any used by modern Cambodians. Indravarman I also constructed the magnificent temples of Preah Ko and Bakong.

The next king, Yasovarman I (A.D. 889–900), built the first "real" city at Angkor, replete with lengthy and flowery inscriptions engraved on many of the buildings. Because of the proliferation of great words, it was thought for years that Yasovarman was also responsible for many of Angkor's great works, including the building of Angkor Wat. Subsequent exploration and evaluation, however, rendered Yasovarman's verbiage hollow.

Angkor's so-called Golden Age did not commence until the beginning of the eleventh century and the rule of King Suryavarman I (A.D. 1001–1050). He built the grand plaza and the palace at Angkor in addition to the great temple of Baphuon.

Angkor Wat ("temple of the capital") was unequivocally the greatest structure in the entire Khmer empire. It was built by King Suryavarman II, who reigned from 1113 to 1150. In political as well as aesthetic terms, the rule of Suryavarman II was the apex of the Khmer civilization, and Angkor Wat was certainly his crowning achievement.

Angkor Wat served during the king's lifetime as a temple and after his death as a tomb. Unlike the other temples in the Angkor area, the main entrance of Suryavarman II's funerary temple faced west (toward the land of the dead).

As was consistent with Khmer tradition, we have no record of the great architect—or architects—who designed this extraordinary temple. We do know that

Each of the Bayon's fifty-four huge towers are intricately sculpted with Jayavarman's Buddha-like image.

Angkor Wat was built with the aid of Indian immigrants, many of whom were Buddhists. And we also know that Angkor Wat was designed as a series of five rectangular and concentric enclosures, each one bringing the worshiper literally closer to the central mountainous pyramid with the tallest shrine. To reach the center of the temple, visitors had to walk along a 1,000-foot (300m) -long engraved causeway; the carvings featured mostly Hindu symbols.

The ancient Khmers built their religious buildings on mountain sites, but subsequent shrines such as Angkor Wat were built on the plains. Angkor Wat's tall, conical towers represented Mount Meru, often referred to as "the Mount Olympus of Hindu cosmology." The great temple's large central tower and the four smaller towers that surround it symbolize Meru's five peaks. These towering "peaks"—some reaching more than 200 feet (60m) high—and spreading terraces lie within a 650-foot (200m) moat that isolated them from the surrounding buildings and countryside. Built on a square base and consisting of nine different levels of stonework, the towers taper as they ascend. All of the unusual shapes were utilized to take full viewing advantage of the vaunted "local light" in this part of Cambodia.

The outer wall was said to represent the mountains at the world's edge, and the moat was symbolic of the oceans beyond. This reinforced the feeling that the Khmer temples were set apart from all other aspects of the everyday lives of the people, providing them with expansive, contemplative places where they could peacefully venerate their dead kings.

The carved reliefs found throughout Angkor Wat chronicled both secular and divine history and can be perceived as guides to heaven and hell. The details on the walls of the temple teem with intricate, elegant renderings of plants, leaves, and dragons and other mystical creatures, in addition to *devatas* (divinities) and *apsaras* (nymphs, or half-naked temple dancers). Also found on the temple walls is a king mounted on an elephant with a fly whisk in his hand and an emperor leading his troops into battle.

Of particular note were the drawings around the gallery on the temple's first level, some of which wrapped around to Angkor Wat's outer terrace and rose up to a height of about eight feet (2.4m). Many of these subtle, shallow-relief carvings portrayed tales from Indian mythology, especially the *Mahabarata* and the *Ramayana*. Other designs depicted incidents from the life and times of King Suryavarman II.

The architects of Angkor Wat combined ancient as well as new construction techniques of the time, many of which were surprisingly advanced for their day. The masonry was joined by iron dowels, not mortar, and the entire structure was held together mainly by precision engineering facilitated by gravity. Although the temple itself had a relatively flimsy foundation, the structure was so well balanced that it has remained standing and in excellent condition to this day.

Angkor Wat's structural similarity to the eighth-century pyramidal temples at Palenque has generated speculation that the building methods used in the Mayan and the Khmer cultures were derived from an earlier Asian "super" culture, of which both were possibly offshoots. This theory remains entirely speculative, however, since this mega-culture disappeared under mysterious circumstances, with no palpable record at all.

The galleries and corridors of Angkor Wat were precisely aligned to the directions of the compass, in

The walls of Angkor Wat teem with elegant renderings of both a divine and secular nature, including devatas (divinities) and apsaras (nymphs, or half-naked dancers).

AYERS ROCK

Mystical Wonder of the Outback

The Rock (previous page), 2,844 feet (865m) high and six miles (9.6km) around, has been described by the Aborigines as "a place where the dreaming comes up, right from inside the ground."

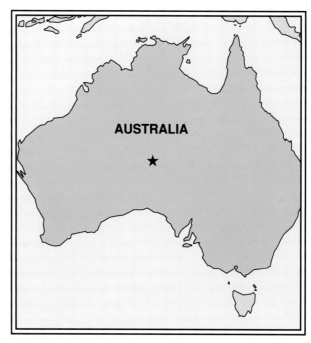

AUSTRALIA

Describing the natural wonders of the world usually results in an exercise in superlatives. The *incredible* Himalayas, stretching for two thousand miles (3,200km), are the *highest* mountains on earth. *Astonishing* Victoria Falls, one of the planet's most *dramatic* and *picturesque* waterfalls, plunges into a mile-deep (1.6km) chasm. The Grand Canyon, one of the oldest natural formations, offers a *sensational* vista of geological history and sheer, *awe-inspiring* splendor.

What, then, can be said about a single rock sitting in the middle of the Australian desert? How can a rock—a mere pebble when compared to Everest—be grouped with the acknowledged marvels of our planet?

Ayers Rock is a subtler phenomenon. It may not rank as a mountain, but to counter any misconceptions or disparaging comments about its size, it is a monolith. Rising in an abrupt, essentially straight ascent off the flat floor of the plain, Ayers Rock reaches a height of 2,844 feet (865m), which is sufficient to reward hardy visitors who've made the climb with a hundred-mile (160km) view in all directions. Its girth, too, is considerable—some six miles (9.6km) around in a roughly ovoid shape. A couple of hours are required to circumvent the rock on foot—that is, if one doesn't stop to look at its many grottoes and formations (more about that in a moment). As such, Ayers qualifies as the *biggest* rock mass in the world, not an inconsiderable claim.

Geologically, Ayers Rock (or simply "the Rock" as contemporary Australians call it) represents the only remaining pinnacle of a once-eminent chain of mountains located miles away. Millions of years of erosion have produced a unique formation of sedimentary rock made up of feldspar, quartz, sandstone, mica, magnetite, and brown and red oxides of iron. The process of erosion, in fact, is ongoing. Known as spalling, layers are sloughed off in the form of flakes, much as a snake sheds its skin. The Rock, however, doesn't lose its distinctive shape. The color, too, is in flux. The Rock usually looks reddish brown, but the changing light of the sun and interplay of clouds alter its complexion and the resulting hues range from pink or scarlet in the morning to a more shimmery orange in the late blaze of sunset; purple and steel gray are not unheard of.

Permanent pools of water glisten on the Rock's flat top, and when heavy rains occur, hundreds of waterfalls, some as high as 700 feet (215m), appear suddenly in the cracks and crevices, and their cascades make the massif come to life. Ayers Rock has even been known to emit a strange noise, a whistling or moaning sound that scientists attribute to the action of thermal winds created by the release of the rock's stored heat. Additional noises come from the wild animals—dingoes (wild dogs), kangaroos, and wallabies—who inhabit the site. They prowl and frolic before dawn and after dusk, when the tourists aren't around and the rock once again stands sentinel in the desert darkness, reclaiming its private self.

Ayers Rock is located almost smack-dab in the middle of the Australian continent, in the state known as the Northern Territory, about 800 miles (1,280km) south of Darwin, 1,230 miles (1,970km) from Perth on Australia's southwest coast, and an equal distance from Sydney and Melbourne in the southeast. This is Australia's famed "Outback," its "Dead Heart," or "Red Center," a generally unpopulated area of land marked by sand, scrub brush, and parched earth that encompasses thousands of square miles. The nearest town, about 250 miles (400km) away, is Alice Springs, the "Alice" that achieved some fame in Nevil Shute's World War II novel, *A Town Like Alice*.

Although the rock itself was first seen from afar by European settlers in 1872, a big salt flat known as Lake Amadeus kept them from getting any closer. A year later, William Gosse, a deputy surveyor general, approached from another direction and scrutinized the rock up close. He felt it was "the most wonderful natural feature I have ever seen" and named it after Sir Henry Ayers, Australia's premier at the time. Today, the rock is part of the Uluru National Park, a reserve set aside for Australia's native population, the Aborigines.

The changing light of the sun and the movement of the clouds alter the Rock's complexion hourly— from pink to orange to steel gray.

Permanent pools of water glisten on the Rock's flat top, and when heavy rains occur, hundreds of water-falls appear in the massif's cracks and crevices.

It is the rich, diverse mythology of the Aborigines that gives the rock its mystical, mysterious significance. As a member of the Pitjantjatjara Aborigines told a writer not long ago, "This is not a rock; it is my grand-father. This is a place where the dreaming comes up, right up from inside the ground." While it may seem odd for someone to refer to an inanimate object as family, Aborigines know no such inhibitions, for their mythology and religious customs allow room for the supernatural (although they probably wouldn't call it that). Magic is performed, for example, and medicine men have prominent roles and great status in the tribes. But central to their beliefs and customs are the concepts of "the dreaming" and "the Dreamtime."

The dreaming refers to what anthropologists have described as the "creative past"—the myths and rit-uals followed and handed down, orally, from genera-tion to generation. Continuity with this past is consid-ered highly important, so much so that it figures in initiation rites and is the province of tribal elders whose authority is absolute.

The Dreamtime, meanwhile, is the name for an early period of history when the earth was still being formed and was inhabited by part-animal, part-human crea-tures called, for example, "carpet snake people." During the Dreamtime, these nomadic ancestors of today's Aborigines journeyed across the desert, surviving in the harsh wilderness by finding watering holes and other "soaks" where water would collect. Knowledge of these routes—particularly the location of the water sources—is part of the lore that has been passed down over the years and guides the Aborig-ines of today in their own wanderings. Ayers Rock is one such stop along the Dreamtime trails.

For the Pitjantjatjara, Ayers Rock also marks a spot that serves as the center of their universe. Because the rock is believed to have been created by mythical beings working with a very deliberate design and purpose, every crack, bump, and outcropping is con-sidered sacred. One Pitjantjatjara legend holds that a tribe of carpet snake people who had settled at the Uluru water hole were attacked by an evil tribe of snake men. At the end of the battle that ensued, a huge monolith burst out of the desert floor—Ayers Rock, the Aborigines' Uluru. This and another battle that is said to have occurred in the same vicinity have found their way into songs, fables, and ceremonies still in use today.

Other aboriginal myths address various compo-nents of the sacred, chameleonic rock. For example, a water hole that sits at the foot of the monolith is said to have come from the blood of a carpet snake man who died in the Dreamtime conflict with the snake men. Likewise, one piece of stone sticking out of the facade is thought to be the severed nose of an evil snake warrior. A large, gaping cave was created, according to legend, from the mouth of a grief-stricken woman who was crying over the loss of her son in battle.

And there's more. Holes in the rock are the eyes of another dead enemy or they are symbols of the holes made by women using digging sticks to forage for food or of the barrage of arrows loosed upon the tribe during battle. Impressions in one cave that look like footprints were made by ancestors fleeing a devil dingo. A rock in another cave represents a sleeping Dreamtime elder. A fold in another part of the rock looks to the Aborigines like Kandju, the sand lizard, who came to Uluru to look for the boomerang of light. Non-Aborigines have gotten into the act as well: they've dubbed some markings and grooves on the north face "the Skull" for their resemblance to a human head.

Not all of the Rock's features are allegorical in nature. Through the years, Aborigines have added cave paintings and engravings of their own—some with fertility images, others depicting the local flora and fauna, still others representing important common-place activities such as an emu hunt. Inscriptions in one rock tunnel have to do with tribal initiation rites. Known as the "hare-wallaby cave of Mala," this cave may have been where novices in elaborate head-dresses were shown the sacred "ritual pole" for the first time and where they pledged their obedience to tribal law to the sound of loud, chanting approval from the elders. It is one of several parts of Uluru considered so sacred that they are kept off limits to non-Aborigines.

Another taboo holds that men may not enter the caves of women—and vice versa—for fear of certain death. One cave that is off-limits to men is the fertility cave visited by pregnant women. Off-limits to women and uninitiated males is a cave containing a stain on the wall that is said to be the original blood from a Dreamtime ritual. An attendant story involves a wo-man who was gathering fruit from a fig tree just outside this cave more than a hundred years ago. Spotted by an elder, she became so frightened that she fled, only to be tracked down and killed after a tribal council ruled she had profaned the gods.

Those hikers hardy enough to make the steep climb are rewarded with a hundred-mile (160km) view in all directions.

New Lease on Aboriginal Life

THE PITJANTJATJARA ABORIGINES' MYSTICAL LINKS TO Ayers Rock go back to the Dreamtime, the earliest days of human existence. Of more recent vintage is a legal agreement with the Australian government, which was reached in 1983 after many years of negotiating, and grants the tribe freehold title to Uluru National Park. Given the Aborigines' sad, troubled history in modern Australia, many believe that the arrangement is a major milestone.

The Pitjantjatjara were among the five hundred or so Aboriginal tribes whose populations were decimated in the century and a half following the arrival of European settlers in Australia in 1788. These newcomers—ranchers, miners, and others—set up towns and farms and in the process laid claims to what had been Aboriginal lands, employing the force of arms when they felt it necessary. Not surprisingly, the weaker natives were stunned and routed, their lives disrupted in many ways.

First and foremost, their traditional nomadic life-styles were threatened by the encroachment of settlements into the wilderness that had been theirs for thousands of years. The Aborigines, needing work and food, became virtual slaves if they accepted work and paupers if they did not. They contracted diseases for which they had no immunities and, as dark-skinned people, suffered humiliating racial discrimination. Clashes over land, cattle, and sheep were frequent and bloody.

Certainly some of the Aborigines were able to avoid death or destitution, and not all the settlers ran roughshod over them, but generally speaking, their way of life was more than supplanted; it was nearly trampled to death. By 1934, the Aborigines numbered just 50,000, down from roughly 350,000 in 1788, and most observers were predicting their eventual extinction. More than two hundred years later, they still have not fully recovered.

Some progress has been accomplished lately, however. Protective legislation had been enacted in the late nineteenth century, but measures strong enough to make a difference in health, education, and employment weren't adopted until the 1930s. In the 1960s, Australians went further and eliminated discriminatory language from the country's constitution and set up the Office of Aboriginal Affairs. In addition, the federal government was empowered to pass legislation concerning the Aborigines, whereas prior to that, power had resided with the individual states, which had inhibited coordinated nationwide action.

As a result of these and other developments, the Aborigines' population decline was reversed. Figures from the late 1970s showed that there were about 40,000 full-bloods and 100,000 mixed-bloods and concluded that numbers were expected to double by the year 2000. Problems remain, of course, just as they do in the United States and Canada with their native populations. Still, the hope is that integration—especially economic integration and equal opportunity—can be achieved.

The Ayers Rock agreement with the Pitjantjatjara was one of the more visible attempts made by the Australian government to attain that goal and to atone for wrongs committed in the past. According to its terms, the Aborigines lease the park back to the government, and both parties share any revenues generated by tourism (about 100,000 people visit the site yearly). Just as important, the Aborigines also constitute a majority on the site's board of management.

Few Australians—native or immigrant—could have remained unmoved by the ceremony in which Ayers Rock was restored to its original owners. A newspaper headline offered this brief but heartfelt sentiment: "Ayers Rock Is White Man's Dreaming, Too."

With links to the Rock and the surrounding land dating back to the earliest days of human civilization, the Aboriginal people (right) have only recently been able to reverse centuries of disease, discrimination, and decline.

© Sarah Keyt/Envision

Yet another story centers around a spot where a dingo died after a fight with a kangaroo. Since the dingo had died an honorable death—during a hunting expedition—the spot thus became the place from which a spirit known as *kurapunyi* is summoned by the elders of the Mulga-seed clan. They do so when someone in the tribe thinks that one of their clan has been stricken dead by magic visited upon them by another tribe. When the elders want to inflict revenge, mulga bushes are placed on either side of the so-called kurapunyi stone with the leaves pointing in the direction they wish the evil magic to go. The stone is then rubbed while calling upon the ritual dingo to "go smell out the guilty one and destroy him." The dingo "travels" under the earth, performs his ascribed deed, and then returns to the stone at Ayers Rock.

Call it sorcery. Call it voodoo. Call it what you will. To the scientific twentieth-century mind, Ayers Rock is a fascinating, beautiful natural wonder. But to the Aborigines, the rock is Uluru, the place where the Dreamtime—past, present, and future—merges and becomes one.

Ayers Rock (above) has never lost its distinctive shape despite the ongoing process of erosion called spalling, where layers of the Rock's "skin" are sloughed off in the form of flakes.

MACHU PICCHU

City in the Sky

High above the Urubamba River in the Peruvian Andes, the ancient Incas created the man-made marvels of Machu Picchu (previous page). Although they never learned to make iron tools, the Incas were masters of arts and crafts, as evidenced by the exquisite jewelry and ceramic artifacts (below) found at Machu Picchu (right and opposite) and elsewhere. They were also ranked among history's greatest architects and planners; without pack animals, they figured out how to transport great stones over long distances and up dizzying heights.

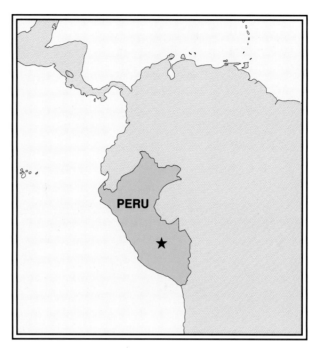

Perched high on a cliff between two peaks in the Peruvian Andes, Machu Picchu appears to be a classic, impregnable mountaintop citadel. Dominating the hills and valleys for miles around, its massive, sophisticated stone structures and fortifications would seem more than enough to put the fear of God into any and all neighboring tribes and would-be conquerors. What, then, caused it to be abandoned? Was its fate a localized phenomenon, or was it tied to that of the Incas, one of the most powerful people ever to rule in South America?

This enigmatic empire first drew Hiram Bingham, a Yale University archaeologist, to Peru in 1911. He went there in search of Vilcabamba, the long-sought "lost city" of the Incas, where Manco Capac and his surviving followers had fled in 1536 after being routed from their capital, Cuzco, by the Spanish. Bingham began his forays in the Urubamba River gorge, seventy miles (112km) northwest of Cuzco, and wandered the valleys looking for pottery shards or other signs of previous human settlement, but the dense jungle of Peru was reluctant to yield any of its secrets.

After a few days of meandering in vain, Bingham met a peasant farmer who told him of some ruins on a nearby hillside known locally as Machu Picchu, or "old peak." An excited Bingham was led through the thick brush and across several rickety rope bridges to a stunning hilltop setting. There, poking through the moss and other vegetation that blanketed the site, Bingham discovered, or rediscovered, the beautiful remains of white granite stone walls and other remarkable pieces of architecture. As he later wrote, "Dimly, I began to realize that this wall with its adjoining semicircular temple over the cave were as fine as the finest stonework in the world. . . . It fairly took my breath away. What could this place be?"

It was not Vilcabamba. Archaeologists who followed in Bingham's footsteps finally found that fabled locale many miles away. No, this was the site now known worldwide by the same name local farmers had always used: Machu Picchu. No written records have been found to enable archaeologists to identify it any more precisely. Not even the Spanish, known to have scrupulously recorded all the details of the towns they were about to pillage and subdue, committed the words *Machu Picchu* to their savage scrolls.

Historians take this to mean that it was just one town in an outlying part of the empire, and a relatively small one by Incan standards, home to just one thousand people. (The Incas ruled over an empire of about six million.) But it is precisely because of its anonymity and its physical isolation that Machu Picchu was able to remain so well preserved for nearly four hundred years. It is now a justifiably renowned site where one can glimpse, in microcosm, the fascinating and strange life of the Incas. However, even though Machu Picchu has been laid bare to the eyes of tourists and others, many of its mysteries remain unsolved, the topic of often heated discussion and wild speculation.

When the site was cleared so that formal research could commence during a second Bingham expedition a year later, Machu Picchu began to fully reveal its many wonders. The 10,000-foot (3,000m) -high ruins consisted of roughly 200 rooms or buildings within an area covering approximately 400 by 325 yards (360 by 295m). Cliffs and mountains girded the town on three sides, and a man-made stone wall enclosed the fourth.

Today, the sound of rushing water, rising two thousand feet (600 m) from the valley, mixes with the cries of condors soaring on Andean gusts. Clouds, mist, and fog often blanket the site. The vast, forbidding Amazon jungle begins not far away. In this stark milieu, the Incas worked all manner of architectural marvels.

The Incas are known to have mastered the art of smelting and alloying soft metals, as evidenced by the profusion of exquisite gold, silver, copper, and bronze jewelry and artifacts found at Machu Picchu and elsewhere. But they never figured out how to make iron tools—which is not so strange in and of itself but is baffling when trying to discern how they worked the hard rock into grand temples, palaces, terraces, fountains, stairs, water basins, channels, houses, and the other great edifices of Machu Picchu.

Some have claimed that meteoric hematite was used, but this theory is considered unlikely due to the sheer amount of construction that was done. Machu Picchu would have to have been deluged by frequent, inordinately heavy meteor showers.

Other theories were given consideration. Could the Incas have been helped by extraterrestrial visitors wielding laser drills and chisels or were other, occult forces employed against the stones? It is a measure of Machu Picchu's mysterious magnitude that such speculations are even offered.

It should be emphasized, too, that the Incas were ranked among history's greatest architects. Indeed, it has been said that the "grandiose concept of its cities and the handling of rock mass finds no rival in either the New World or the Old." For instance, the stones that make up the buildings at Machu Picchu fit together so closely—no mortar was used—that even today, after the ravages of time and the many earth-

quakes that have plagued the region, a knife blade cannot be run between them.

Equally astounding, the Incas did not have draft animals to shoulder the many burdens of construction on such a grand scale. Yet stone had to be transported over long distances and up dizzying heights. The site's natural outcrop of rock had to be lopped off and flattened for the town's foundation. Fertile soil from the valley below had to be brought up the steep hillsides to fill the newly built farming terraces. However, there is no mystery as to how this labor was performed. The use of slaves—captured tribes and the Incan lower classes—adds a staggering, tragic human dimension to the glory that is Machu Picchu. Their job was made more difficult by another anomaly of Incan technology: they had not yet discovered the wheel.

So what was Machu Picchu? A typical Incan town? A temple complex? An elaborate observatory? A home of the Incan ruling classes? A sanctuary for the "Virgins of the Sun" (the Incas were sun worshipers)? A fortified outpost for keeping tabs on the tribes of the jungle? A resort? All of these roles have been postulated, and evidence has been gathered to support each of the interpretations.

It is perhaps easiest to imagine Machu Picchu as a ceremonial place of religious or mystical significance. One of the most prominent items on display is the *Intihuatana*, the sacred stone central to Incan worship. The Intihuatana, which means "hitching post of the sun" in Quechua, the Indian language still spoken today, is dedicated to Inti, the powerful sun god, and was used by Incan high priests to observe the movements of the sun and moon, to chart the seasons, and to determine solstices and equinoxes. It was also used as a sundial. In one ceremony at the solstice mark-

The stones used in the construction of the buildings at Machu Picchu (top left) fit together so closely (detail, bottom left)—without the use of mortar—that a knife blade cannot be run between them.

© Lee Kuhn/FPG International

ing the onset of winter, the god Inti was symbolically "hitched" to the Intihuatana as a way of beseeching him to return and grant the Incas another summer.

Inti, a deity of life and fertility, was not the primary Incan god, just the most popular. The chief deity was Viracocha, the god of creation. Additional gods in the Incan pantheon included those of the stars, moon, thunder, and the planet Venus; each had his own cult and attendant priestess, who was known as a Chosen Woman. Other Incan religious practices thought to have occurred at Machu Picchu include human sacrifices (possibly only in times of trouble), as well as the

Evidence has been gathered that lends support to several interpretations of the possible roles Machu Picchu played: it could have been a typical Incan town, a temple complex, an elaborate observatory, a fortified outpost, or maybe even a resort.

reading of slaughtered llamas and vicunas' entrails to predict the rains and harvests.

No analysis of entrails, it seems safe to say, would have forecast a quick collapse for an empire whose influence at its height extended some 2,300 miles (3,680km) from the southern border of present-day Colombia to central Chile. But swift it was.

In 1527, the death of the Incan leader, Huayna Capac, set off a succession battle between two of his five hundred (!) sons that embroiled the Incas in a devastating civil war. Five years later, one of the sons, Atahualpa, prevailed, but at the cost of an even greater threat: a conquistador by the name of Francisco Pizarro. Pizarro and his men landed at coastal Tumbes on May 13, 1532, determined to subdue the Incas in much the same way that his fellow countryman Hernan Cortes had conquered the Aztecs and Mayans in present-day Mexico and Guatemala just over ten years earlier.

News that the Spanish had inflicted devastating damage in the north was not known to the Incas. Historians say the Incas were so rife with dissension at this point that it wouldn't have mattered anyway. As it happened, Pizarro's cavalry and gunpowder proved much too awesome for Incan foot soldiers armed with bows and arrows. Atahualpa himself was taken prisoner and subsequently executed. The shocked Incas became submissive, and the Spanish conquerors had themselves an easy victory, greatly increasing their holdings in the New World. Some of the tattered Incas who survived the initial Spanish onslaught held on for another few years in Vilcabamba, the legendary town that had first beckoned Hiram Bingham.

Strangely, the Spaniards appear to have bypassed Machu Picchu. No evidence of arson, pillage, or mass

Although the conquistador Francisco Pizzaro subdued the Incan people throughout South America, it is likely that he and his soldiers never set foot in Machu Picchu.

Neruda's *Heights of Machu Picchu*

The Incas who built what the poet Neruda called the "high city of laddered stones" had no written language, so it's been left to contemporary scientists and poets to interpret the meaning of Machu Picchu.

SINCE THEIR "REDISCOVERY" IN 1911, THE SPECTACULAR ruins of Machu Picchu have worked their cryptic charm on tens of thousands of archaeologists, historians, backpackers, occultists, New Agers, and other tourists from all over the world. For some, the visit has been part of their work; for others, a vacation destination rivaling the Acropolis in Greece. For Pablo Neruda (1904–1973), the Latin American poet who won the Nobel Prize for Literature in 1971, the arduous journey to Machu Picchu was a pilgrimage.

"For me, Peru has been the womb of America, an arena encircled by high and mysterious stones," said Neruda just before his visit to the site in 1943. He was returning home to his native Chile after serving for three years as his government's consul in Mexico. (It is not uncommon for Latin American writers to enter the diplomatic corps.) But the stopover was more than a simple matter of geographic convenience. Machu Picchu was not just on the way; it was a logical destination for a poet who was developing a broad vision of Latin American history and politics, one that was inevitably linked with the fate of the continent's native peoples and the Spanish conquest.

Neruda had spent much of the previous decade in Spain, acquainting himself with the life, language, and literature of Latin America's "mother country." The rise of fascism in Spain and the Spanish Civil War—the dual horrors that had recently scarred that country—couldn't help but scar the young poet as well. Neruda subsequently traveled to Cuba, Guatemala, and the United States in an attempt to learn more about and gain further insight into the South American hybrid—part Indian, part Spanish. "I thought about ancient American man," he once said. "I saw his ancient struggles linked with present struggles."

Anyone visiting Machu Picchu cannot remain unaware of the human cost involved in the building of the grand structures, the excruciating labor required to lift and shape the massive stones to such exactitude. Likewise, it is not difficult to imagine the austere living conditions that prevailed on an Andean mountaintop in the sixteenth century: the harsh weather, the scarcity of tillable land, and the generally oppressive nature of the feudal Incan society. Neruda took this all to heart and filtered it through his unique sensibility.

© Lee Kuhn/FPG International

The resulting work was one of his most powerful poems and a landmark in twentieth-century Latin American literature, the epic *Altura de Machu Picchu* (*Heights of Machu Picchu*).

Neruda used the following words (from the poem's sixth canto) to describe the site:

Then on the ladder of the earth I climbed
through the lost jungle's tortured thicket
up to you, Machu Picchu.
High city of laddered stones . . .

Mother of stone, spume of condors.

High reef of the human dawn.

Spade lost in the primal sand.

This was the dwelling, this is the place:
here the broad grains of maize rose up
and fell again like red hail.

Here gold thread came off the vicuna
to clothe lovers, tombs, and mothers,
king and prayers and warriors. . . .

In the poem's twelfth and final canto, Neruda offered a dramatic declaration of solidarity with the long-dead Incas whose lives he encountered at Machu Picchu:

Rise to be born with me, brother.

Give me your hand out of the deep
region seeded by all your grief. . . .

Fasten your bodies to me like magnets.
Hasten to my veins to my mouth.
Speak through my words and my blood.

destruction—the customary Spanish calling cards—was found at the site. In fact, some scholars believe the city was abandoned and empty of people well before the Spaniards arrived in Peru. How, then, did the vital town of Machu Picchu cease to exist?

Malaria is one tropical killer that may have done the job. An epidemic of some other sort is also a possibility. In such an insular community, disease could have spread quickly and lethally. Bingham found one skeleton of a rich woman bearing signs of another potential killer—syphilis. One surmises she could not have been the only person in Machu Picchu to suffer, though it is hard to imagine an entire town succumbing.

Other theories focus on Machu Picchu's religious nature. Commentaries on Inca customs written in the sixteenth century by Garcilaso de Vega, who was the son of a mixed marriage between an Inca princess and a Spaniard, recorded that if any one of the sacred Virgins of the Sun were defiled, "servants, relatives, and neighbors, inhabitants of the same town and their cattle were all killed. No one was left. . . . The place was damned and excommunicated so that no one could find it, not even the animals." A harsh fate, to be sure, but not so outlandish for a sun-worshiping mecca such as Machu Picchu. Finally, so as not to overlook the obvious, one must also consider what happens in a town filled with virgins: zero birth rate.

The short life of Machu Picchu has given rise to some of the greatest mysteries known to man. Perhaps the most poignant one of all is that the Incas had no written language—no cuneiform, no hieroglyphics—for us to decipher. There are no Incan Dead Sea Scrolls, only the silent yet eloquent ruins such as those at Machu Picchu.

CERNE ABBAS

The Chalk Giant

Pagan image or Christian icon, Hercules or Herculean figure, evidence suggests that this enormous chalk giant of Cerne Abbas (previous page) may be nearing its two-thousandth birthday.

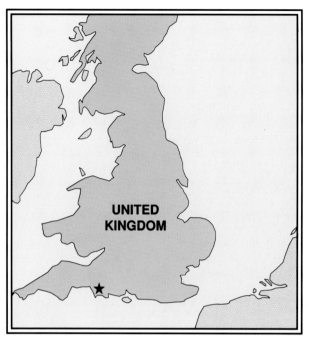

UNITED KINGDOM

It is certainly the largest—and probably the most anatomically explicit—rendering of a naked man ever carved into a hillside. And it's possible that this fertility symbol has survived nearly two thousand years virtually intact.

The shifting winds and driving rains of England's Dorset County have washed away, however, any other telling symbols—including letters or numbers—that could have further explained or helped to identify the 180-foot (55m) chalk giant of Cerne Abbas. Scientific speculation and local gossip abound with possibilities, specifically that there were at least three letters (and perhaps several numbers as well) etched between the giant's feet.

Some say the actual "name" of the giant was once engraved in the earth. Others suggest that there was a simple "ANO" (for *anno domini*) written in chalk, along with a date—probably 1748—when the huge figure was recut. The most likely explanation is that there was one of several three-lettered inscriptions: IHS (which referred to Jesus), IAO (which stood for Jehovah), or JHD (which signified the cryptic Latin expression, *Jehovah/Jesus hoc destruxit*, "God has overthrown this"). The latter phrase was reportedly interpreted as a response by monks who wished to dilute the giant's potent pagan imagery.

While the brazen symbolism of its erect phallus—in addition to the delineated nipples and ribs—seems blatantly representative of a figure of fertility, there are several other colorful theories on the significance and origins of this not-exactly-sleeping giant.

One ancient legend contends that the chalk was merely used to outline the presence of a corpse—much as police do today. No matter, of course, that the deceased was a 180-foot (55m) giant with a 45-foot (14m) shoulder span and was holding a 121-foot (37m) knobbed club in his mammoth right hand. This tale tells of a giant who had apparently been terrorizing the local shepherds by devouring their sheep and causing all sorts of other mayhem and destruction. One day when the giant lay down on the hillside to digest his most recent meal and fell asleep, the locals killed him and drew a chalk outline around his lifeless body. As to what purpose that might have served, we don't know—perhaps as a warning to other sheep-eating giants not to mess with the folks of Cerne Abbas. But, alas, like many ancient fables that have come to us through the ages, it has not been equipped with a tidy moral.

Another legend has it that the giant of Cerne Abbas really represented the mythical strongman Hercules. An identifiable depiction of a naked, club-wielding Hercules was found on a fragment of Romano-British earthenware in Norfolk. As additional proof that the giant of Cerne Abbas indeed cut a Herculean figure, archaeologists cite the presence of a Hercules cult in Britain—an offshoot of a secret Roman society devoted to the worship of the famed Greek hero under the Emperor Commodus, who ruled from A.D. 180 to 193. The Cerne Abbas giant may have been the Celtic equivalent of Hercules. Also, this giant was often referred to as Helith, Helis, or Heil—any of which could be a bastardization of Hercules.

A carving found in Sweden dating back to the Bronze Age has generated some well-founded speculation with its image of a naked man holding a spear in his right hand. This carving most likely represents the Scandinavian war god and fertility figure, Tiwaz. Perhaps it is Tiwaz whose Celtic stand-in might right now be stretched out on the hills of Cerne Abbas in Great Britain.

Although the wind and rain of England's Dorset County may have washed away any identifying numbers or letters, it remains obvious that the great chalk giant of Cerne Abbas was a symbol of fertility.

Most often called the Long Man of Wilmington—but also known as the Lone Man, the Lanky Man, or when untended, the Green Man—this 231-foot (70.2m) outline of a human figure has been identified as Mercury, Mohammed, St. Paul, or some anonymous ancient surveyor.

Whoever he was or was supposed to be, the giant's rendering was almost assuredly created by digging away the soil, exposing the white chalk underneath. And while we have not yet been able to precisely date the image of the naked giant, it is obvious that the locals have been diligent with their upkeep—constantly cleaning and scouring it through the ages.

The first definitive written record is attributed to a letter penned by historian and author John Hutchins in 1751, seven years after publication of his *History of Dorset*. Speaking of the Cerne Abbas giant, Hutchins wrote: "I have heard from the steward of the manor it is a modern thing, cut out in Lord Holles's time [between 1641 and 1666]." It is equally likely, however, that Lord Holles was involved only in the recutting or scouring of the figure and not necessarily in its creation.

Several factors, including the Hercules/Tiwaz connection mentioned previously, would seem to indicate more ancient origins for the giant, in addition to the other hill figures (see sidebar on page 70). Some contend that the proximity of the Trendle—a small earthen enclosure encircled by ditches that *has* been determined as belonging to the Iron Age—is some measure of proof.

The Trendle, which is also referred to locally as the Frying Pan, sits directly above the giant's head, with the knobbed club virtually pointing to it. Until recent times, the Trendle was the literal hub of May Day fertility festivities, where townspeople would pull up a fir tree, dub it a maypole, and then dance around it. It is not likely that most contemporary May Day celebrants would connect the joyful circling of a tree in the park with a do-si-do around a thirty-foot (9m) phallus.

Fertility rites and rituals are ubiquitous in British folklore. Most of these customs have pagan roots, but there have been a number of carvings found on several Christian churches—of naked men and women in full, graphic display—that some contemporary clergy might label as pornographic. In ancient times, there was no such labeling; a naked figure—even one of such magnitude—would not have been deemed obscene. (Most assume that these church carvings dealt with fertility, but again, there has been no definitive explanation as yet.)

While it may seem farfetched, there has been speculation that the giant itself was an outgrowth of the commingling of pagan and Christian beliefs. Some have contended that the monks themselves cut the fertility figure into the earth—perhaps to counteract the raw power of the image, or even, it has been suggested, as a monkish joke made about the abbot's habits.

There were many more-grounded tales of young and old wives sitting on or rubbing up against special stones in order to facilitate fecundity. Certain holy wells, presumably filled with holy water, were also reputed to cure childlessness. Yet few of these touchstones or wells were thought to be as effective as the giant of Cerne Abbas. No doubt an erect thirty-foot (9m) penis was a large part of its allure.

Barren women would travel to the land of this giant and lay for the night within its chalk outline, or come just to sit on the phallus—all in the hopes of becoming pregnant. No doubt some men and women lay down on the giant together, *usually* to facilitate conception.

Whether the giant is celebrating its two-thousandth birthday, or only its three-hundredth, the remarkable thing is how well it has worn through the centuries. No doubt it has been recut at least once, perhaps many, many times.

Tale of the (Land's) Tape

UFFINGTON WHITE HORSE (right)

Location: Two miles (3.2km) south of Uffington village in Oxfordshire, one-quarter mile (400m) northeast of the Iron Age fort of Uffington Castle.

Orientation: Faces northwest on a slope of thirty degrees.

Length: About 360 feet (110m) from nose to tail.

Alias: The Dragon.

Date of Origin: Probably around 100 B.C.

THE GIANT OF CERNE ABBAS (below)

Location: On Giant Hill, one-quarter mile (400m) northwest of Cerne Abbas and eight miles (13km) north of Dorchester.

Orientation: The Giant itself faces west.

Height: 180 feet (55m).

Width: 45 feet (13.7m) across the shoulders.

Outline: The trench is two feet (60cm) wide, 480 yards (438m) around.

Date of Origin: Unknown; possibly around the time of Jesus.

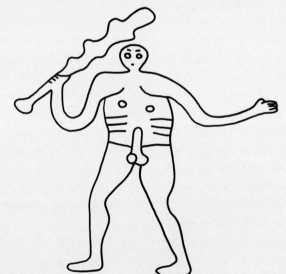

LONG MAN OF WILMINGTON (right)

Location: On the north face of Windover Hill, at the eastern end of the South Downs near Wilmington in Sussex, three miles (5km) north of Eastburne.

Orientation: Faces northeast on a slope of forty degrees.

Speculation: Reputed to be the largest representation of the human figure in the world.

Height (figure): 231 feet (70.2m).

Height (staffs): 232 (70.5m) and 235 feet (71.4m).

Width: Staffs are 115 feet (35m) apart.

Date of Origin: Probably neolithic; roughly 500–100 B.C.

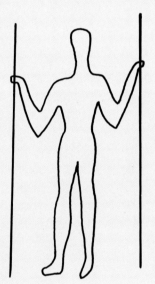

WESTBURY WHITE HORSE (right)

Location: On Bratton Down, two miles (3.2km) from Westbury and one mile (1.6km) southwest from the village of Bratton.

Orientation: The Westbury White Horse faces west on a slope of about fifty degrees.

Villain: Mr. Gee, an eighteenth-century steward, who remodeled the old horse—in the opinion of many—in a soulless and "wretched" fashion.

Height: 108 feet (33m).

Length: 182 feet (55m).

Date of Origin: The "new" one in 1778.

Speculation also ranges widely on the origins of some of the other renowned English hill figures—including the Uffington White Horse in Oxfordshire, the Long Man of Wilmington, and the Westbury White Horse in Wiltshire.

The Uffington White Horse may not be a horse at all, but rather a 365-foot (111m) dragon. Near the stylized chalk outline is Dragon Hill, where St. George is reputed to have slain the dragon. Legend also has it that no grass grows on the hilltop because that's the spot where the dragon's blood was spilled. It is still called the Uffington White Horse, however, and it was most likely created by the Celts during the Iron Age, around 100 B.C. Its proximity to the hillfort of Uffington, which dates back to that time, would confirm this connection. Another argument for the White Horse moniker is that the Celts revered the horse—and deified the animal as the goddess Epona—during this era.

The Long Man of Wilmington is located near neolithic burial mounds, which would probably mean it is more than two thousand years old. Cut into the north face of Windover Hill behind the village of Wilmington in Sussex, this 231-foot (70.2m) figure holds two staffs—232 feet (70.5m) and 235 feet (71.4m) long, respectively—in either hand. Unlike the giant of Cerne Abbas, this rendering lacks any anatomical detail—it's really just an outline. Alternately known as the Lone Man, the Lanky Man, or when untended, the Green Man, the figure has been variously identified as Mercury, Mohammed, St. Paul, a Roman soldier, a Saxon haymaker, and a prehistoric surveyor (who would use the two staffs as sighting poles). Due to its complete lack of sex or any other characteristics (the Long Woman of Wilmington?), it's unlikely that this figure was in any way associated with fertility.

© Cindy A. Pavlinac, M.A.

The Westbury White Horse lies below an Iron Age fort, Bratton Camp, at the edge of Salisbury Plain in Wiltshire. While the Uffington Horse had already garnered considerable attention through the ages, the first mention of a Westbury work was not until 1742, in Reverend Francis Wise's book, *Further Observations on the White Horse and Other Antiquities in Berkshire*, but it was the *original* steed that drew Wise's commentary; that figure, to go by earlier sketches, looked more like a dachshund with a long, thin body, a big eye on its head, and a slim tail (which sounds a bit like the Uffington horse). That horse was destroyed in 1778, and the steward of a local lord remodeled the old, bizarre-looking creature into a perfectly formed, well-defined horse, 182 feet (55m) long and 108 feet (33m) high. If anything, this new White Horse of Westbury was a little too perfect—with critics, then and now, variously calling the artist a "vandal," a "barbarian," and an "unimaginative busybody."

The people of southern England have always taken their hill figures very seriously. They are not only part of the landscape, they have become part of their hearts and souls as well.

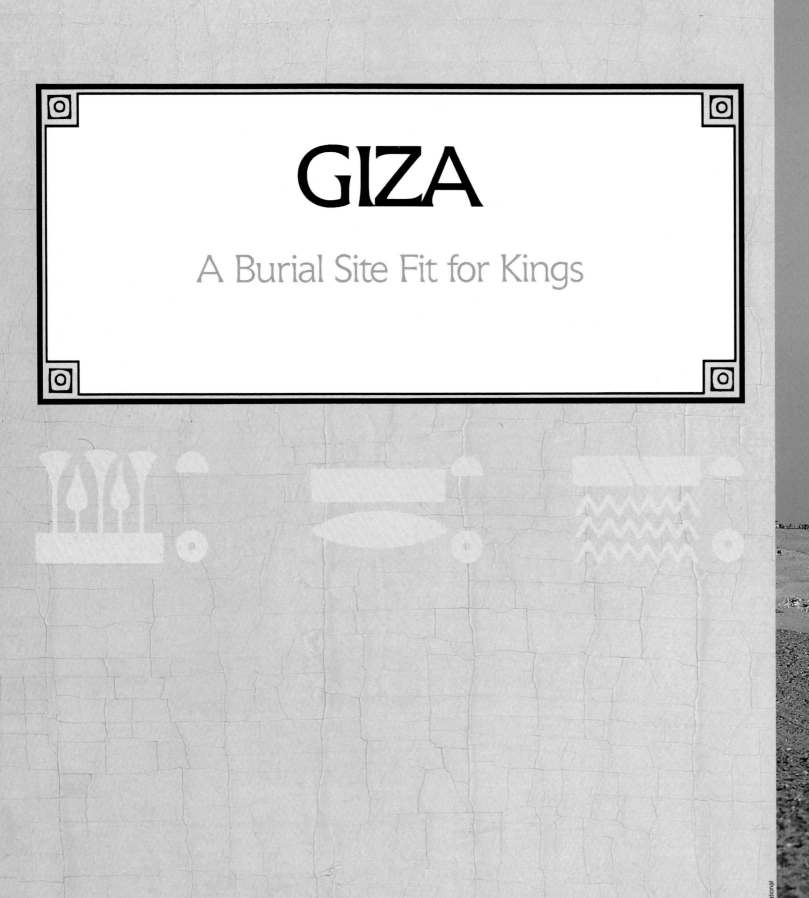

GIZA

A Burial Site Fit for Kings

EGYPT

The Great Pyramid of Cheops, its Egyptian name roughly translated as "Khufu is one belonging to the horizon," is the only one of the Seven Wonders of the Ancient World to have made it into the modern world.

The Great Pyramid was built around 2600 B.C. under the aegis of Cheops (the Greek name for Khufu), the second king of the Fourth Dynasty and the twenty-eighth king of Egypt (if you start counting with Menes). Some archaeologists ascribe the exact date 2608 for Khufu's monumental ground breaking. At that time, upper and lower Egypt had been united under one ruler for about six hundred years, probably beginning with Menes. It was the apex of ancient Egyptian civilization, and the city of Saqqara—home of the Zoser's "step" pyramid, built around 2650 B.C. by the great architect Imhotep—was becoming too densely populated; certainly the cemetery there was becoming overcrowded. So, seeking a suitable setting for a building site—a plateau with an awe-inspiring view—Cheops chose Giza. What had heretofore been a barren, truly deserted desert was to become, over the next five hundred or so years, a burial site for at least two more kings, six queens, and about four thousand elite Egyptians.

Situated northwest of Memphis on the Nile, ten miles (16km) southwest of Cairo, and just north of Saqqara, Giza was to become a massive metropolis of graves, a sprawling "necropolis." For the ancient Egyptians, it was to become the center of their spiritual world, a kingdom of *kas* (souls).

In the great shadow of Cheops' edifice on the Giza plateau in the Nile Valley, two other pyramids were built, one dedicated to Chephren (Khafre in Egyptian) and the other to Mycerinus (Menkaure), as well as dozens of major tombs, including those of Khafre-Ankh, Nefer, Ka-Hief, Nen-Sedjer-Ka, Ka-M-Ankh, and Seshem Nefer I, not to mention the Great Sphinx and the Sphinx temple.

Pharaohs built temples, tombs, and even pyramids in other parts of Egypt—many in the Valley of Kings, where Tutankhamen was buried—but none was as magnificent as Cheops' Great Pyramid in Giza.

These Egyptian kings perceived themselves as living gods who upon their earthly departure would join an underworld populated by other gods. To prepare for this afterlife, the monarchs strategically built their extravagant dwellings between the mighty Nile and the western sky, beneath which the sun disappeared each

Anchored by three great pyramids, all of which were erected as tombs for pharoahs, the Giza plain (previous page) was the spiritual center of the ancient Egyptian world.

night. These "palaces of death" were usually surrounded by smaller tombs to house the servants who would presumably wait upon these deceased monarchs in the afterlife.

Khufu's pyramidic palace originally stood more than 480 feet (146m) high at the topmost stones, which some claim were made of gold. (Compare that to the 555-foot [154m] Washington Monument and the 404-foot [123m] Salisbury Cathedral in England.) It measures just over 756 feet (230m) along each side and contains about two and a half million blocks of limestone; some of the blocks weigh fifteen tons (13.7t).

Much speculation—and considerable awe—has arisen concerning just how the ancient Egyptians managed to construct the mammoth, thirteen-acre (5.2ha) stone configuration with almost pinpoint precision. How did these ancient architects, beginning with the legendary Imhotep, know how to utilize such advanced mathematical calculations?

The Great Pyramid itself differs by no more than eight feet (2.4m) in the lengths of the shortest and longest sides, with its four sides oriented toward the cardinal points of the compass to within less than a tenth of a degree. And incredibly, the pavement that surrounds Khufu's tomb is level to within one inch.

The construction of the Great Pyramid probably took about thirty years, however, there is conjecture that it was completed in a "mere" twenty years. During the process, some four thousand skilled workers—some have tagged the total as closer to one hundred thousand—shaped and placed the stones while tens of thousands of additional laborers were needed for any number of more menial tasks.

The Great Pyramid, built by Cheops around 2600 B.C., is the only Wonder of the Ancient World that has survived.

© Steve Vidler/Leo De Wys Inc.

While many of the stones used to build the pyramids were dug out of the Giza plateau, the Great Sphinx was constructed in what was once a limestone quarry.

The artisans were paid by the king to cut the stones and decorate the tombs with elaborate drawings. The other workers were probably drafted into service during the four months of the year when the Nile flooded and received free room and board for their labors, which consisted primarily of moving two-ton (1.8t) stones from south of the Giza plateau to the pyramid's site. Some Egyptologists have likened this service to the pharaoh to paying taxes today.

The stones used for much of the pyramid were dug out of the Giza plateau itself. The Great Sphinx, the face of which is an outsize representation of King Chephren, was actually constructed in what was once a limestone quarry. The Tura limestone needed for the pyramid's fine facing came from quarries on the eastern side of the Nile. Many of these facing stones were "appropriated" for other projects, including some of Cairo's ancient dwellings. The granite that lined the

Great Pyramid's interior chambers most likely came from Aswan, which is about five hundred miles (800km) up the Nile from Giza.

No one knows precisely how the Egyptian workers transported the huge stones up to the pinnacle of the pyramid. One theory suggests that two rows of men pulled a cart filled with stones over wet logs and up a spiraling side ramp. Another method might have been the use of a ramp built against one face (although the ramp would have had to have been 6,000 feet [1,800m] long to maintain a manageable gradient to the top); once the top stones were set, the ramp was dismantled and white casing stones put in place.

The Great Pyramid, unlike any of the other Egyptian pyramids, had corridors and chambers within its structure. In the center of the north side, just above the base, is an entrance to a small passageway leading down into a chamber in the rock beneath the pyramid. From here, another passageway leads upward to a small chamber, now called the Queen's Chamber, and then to the Grand Gallery, which is 156 feet (47m) long and 28 feet (8.5m) high. The Grand Gallery in turn leads to the largest chamber, the King's Chamber, that contains a sarcophaguslike coffer.

Several millennia passed before the interior of the Great Pyramid was breached by human visitors. Around A.D. 820, interlopers found the ascending passage impassable, due to what they determined were large granite plugs. When they finally reached the King's Chamber, they discovered an empty sarcophagus.

This discovery raised many questions. If the Great Pyramid was not a burial site for the pharaoh, what was its significance? Was it just another temple or monument? If Khufu wasn't buried here, where was his tomb? Or if he was originally buried here, how was his body removed? By whom? And when? Also, who originally blocked the passageway, and why?

At this "unexplained place," there is obviously no shortage of questions, only answers.

Several other questions that have hung over the Nile Valley for nearly four thousand years have been resolved, thanks to a recent find of sixty ancient tombs on the Giza plateau. In fact, some experts have called the find "the most significant archaeological discovery since King Tutankhamen's tomb was opened in 1922."

According to Zahi Hawass, director of the Egyptian Antiquities Organization, this discovery is more significant than old King Tut. "King Tut may be gold," Hawass says, "but this is history."

What made this particular find so significant and historical was that the tombs were not those of kings and queens invariably buried in high style but were burial sites of the so-called little people who built the pyramids.

And what made the discovery even more memorable was that it was made by an anonymous American tourist out for a leisurely horseback ride. After her steed's hoof found a hole in the sand, she dismounted to find the wall of an ancient tomb. In all the ensuing excitement, the woman's name was never recorded, but since her serendipitous accident uncovered the burial places of thousands of anonymous workers, this is probably fitting.

In February 1991, a team of fifteen archaeologists and fifty workers led by Zahi Hawass uncovered the tombs' long-buried secrets: inscriptions, drawings, and food containers as well as the grave sites of "supervisors" and two hundred of their assistants.

© Palnic/Leo De Wys Inc.

Up until that point, no one really knew whether the thousands of workers who toiled for the respective pharaohs were slaves, volunteers, conscripts, or salaried employees. Buried under twenty-four feet (7.3m) of sand, these newly discovered tombs seem to indicate vast numbers of workers—not slaves—whose employment was likely a form of taxation. There is also the first hard evidence that professionals—many of them overseers or directors—supervised these laborers.

Above each tomb were inscriptions, color drawings, and the name of the deceased worker. There were also depictions of the dead person, usually sitting in front of his wife. Between them was a still-life tableau of a table bearing bread and vegetables, then the staple foods in the Egyptian diet.

Most of the tombs had three false entrances, a ruse that apparently was effective in foiling grave despoilers and ultimately allowed archaeologists to find many of the tombs still stocked with sundry valuables, including strings of beads, miniature statues (representing the wives of overseers), and well-preserved pottery.

Also found inside were cone-shaped formations, which presumably housed ancient stores of grain. This turned out to be one of the key tip-offs for modern-day detectives in determining the identities of the deceased.

"Workers in ancient Egypt used to receive their payment in grain," says Hawass. "This proves without doubt that these tombs belonged to Egyptian laborers who built the pyramids."

When it comes to the great tombs and pyramids of Giza, this is one of the few things that one could say with such surety.

Although overshadowed in size by Cheops' Great Pyramid, the tomb of Chefren remains a singularly monumental achievement of design and beauty.

Egyptologists believe that the sixty tombs they dug up were built for those workers who erected the ancient monuments in Giza. If true, says Mark Lehner of the University of Chicago, "it represents the missing silent majority of the people behind the pyramids."

"We know a lot about the royalty and the nobles," says Rita Freed, curator of Egyptian art at Boston's Museum of Fine Arts, "but we know very little about the people who actually made it come to be. [This discovery] tells us how the average man on the street lived and breathed and thought."

Saqqara's First "Step"

THE STEP PYRAMID AT SAQQARA IS A LESS SOPHISTICATED and ambitious structure than the Great Pyramid (or even the two "lesser" ones) built on the Giza plain—and it is also less conventional. The style and shape are quite different than most of the other Egyptian pyramidal monuments that have made it intact (or in theory) through the ages.

This ancient edifice, which contained the tomb of King Zoser of the Third Dynasty, was designed with a series of six steps that made it look as much like a Sumerian ziggurat (or a Mayan temple; see page 108) as an Egyptian pyramid. The king's tomb was submerged underground, beneath a 411-by-358-foot (125-by-109m) base that held a 200-foot (60m) -high step structure.

With the help of the great Imhotep, the visionary architect, king's vizier, sage, sculptor, healer, magician, and all-around Renaissance man, it was conceived and built as part of an expansive funerary compound—the first mortuary complex to be constructed of stone—somewhere between 2650 and 2680 B.C., a solid fifty years *before* the Great Pyramid. Around the king's main monument were chapels, courtyards, and a temple. As was usually the case with Egyptian royalty—and even, as we saw previously, the common folk—King Zoser's tomb was filled with everything he might conceivably have needed in his journey to the next world.

King Zoser's architect, Imhotep, was so respected by his countrymen that he virtually enjoyed the status of a living god in *this* world. Subsequently, some Egyptologists even speculated that there was no flesh-and-blood Imhotep, just an idealized, personified deity. Then, during the large-scale excavation of Saqqara in the 1920s, archaeologists discovered an inscription with a name—not unlike someone writing his or her signature in concrete—near the entrance of the Step Pyramid on

© G. Reitz/Leo De Wys Inc.

the pedestal of a statue of King Zoser. The name was Imhotep.

But where was Imhotep's tomb? Thus far, it has eluded archaeologists, although most students of ancient Egypt assume it is in Saqqara, not far from the great monument he built for his king.

Predating the Great Pyramid by at least fifty years, King Zoser's tomb (above), with its unique series of six steps, looks more like a Mayan temple. Drawings of Egyptian gods often decorated the walls of tombs at Giza. Depicted here (from left) are Khensu (the moon god), Set (the god of war and evil), and Osiris (the judge of the dead).

THE GREAT SERPENT MOUND

The Prehistoric Native American Earthwork

The Great Serpent Mound (previous page), a Native American effigy, snakes for nearly a quarter of a mile (0.4km) in what is now Bratton Township, Ohio.

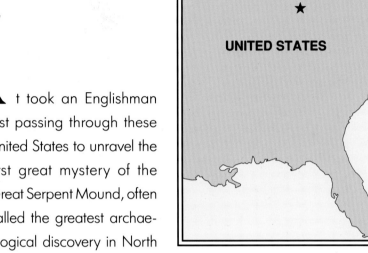

UNITED STATES

It took an Englishman just passing through these United States to unravel the first great mystery of the Great Serpent Mound, often called the greatest archaeological discovery in North America. The mystery revolved around the question of who had built this huge, snake-shaped mound of earth; the Englishman who solved it was Charles Dickens.

In 1842, the renowned author was paddling (in a wheel boat) past another great earthwork near Moundsville, West Virginia, when he theorized that the mounds were made by Native Americans—and not light-skinned biblical characters wiped out in the Great Flood, as was commonly believed at the time.

In his *American Notes*, Dickens worried that the steamboat's whistle might rouse "the extinct tribes who lived so pleasantly here, in their blessed ignorance of white existence, hundreds of years ago." Back then, it was considered blasphemy to think that these "savages" could erect such aesthetically beautiful and symbolically significant structures.

The mounds were considered by many in the New World to be one of the few, if only, links to antiquity, and white settlers were quick to claim them as their own. Yale president Ezra Stiles decided that they were the work of biblical Canaanites—who were also responsible, he said, for founding the temple cultures of Mexico and Peru. Minnesota's Ignatius Donnelly, who was twice an unsuccessful candidate for the vice presidency, proclaimed that the mounds were the work of the few survivors of the lost continent of Atlantis.

Contemporary American writer John G. Mitchell slyly and elegantly provided the Babbitts of East, West, and Middle America with a rationale for their wrongheaded, devout beliefs: "It just wouldn't do to have their creators connected genetically in any way with dusky barbarians. . . . So you stretched the evidence just a little bit and attributed the mound building to lost tribes of Israelites, to wandering Persians or castaway Greeks, to Phoenicians, to Hindus (albeit suntanned, no doubt), to Vikings, to Welshmen, to Irishmen—to anyone, in short, who might be considered by Western European standards a cultural cut or two above the ancestors of Native Americans."

Ironically, the third president of the United States, Thomas Jefferson, was ignored nearly sixty years prior to Dickens' visit when it came to his opinions on this matter. Perhaps one of this country's first archaeologists, Jefferson unearthed about one thousand skele-

other "unexplained place," however, there has been no shortage of speculation.

It was believed at one time that this so-called effigy mound was built to appease the displeased gods who had just unleashed Halley's Comet on the heavens and earth. Bible Belters believed that the oval in the serpent's "mouth" was a sandy stand-in for the apple that Eve planted on Adam. And really true believers contended that the extraordinary earthwork was drawn by the hand of God to signify the Garden of Eden. To these fundamental folks, the twisting mound of clay and rock and soil and sod could be nothing but Eden's evil serpent brought to some huge, terrible manifestation in the American Midwest.

There are at least ten thousand ceremonial and burial mounds of ancient ancestry to be found in the Ohio Valley and perhaps one hundred thousand scattered throughout the United States. Some are built in

This nineteenth-century survey of the Great Serpent Mound (below) was published about seventy years after Thomas Jefferson (left) unearthed one thousand skeletons near his home at Monticello, Virginia, and speculated about the existence of "an Indian monument."

tons from a spheroidal barrow while digging near his home at Monticello, Virginia. In 1781, he wrote: "I know of no such thing existing as an Indian monument . . . Unless indeed it be the barrows of which many are to be found all over the country.

"That they were repositories of the dead," Jefferson continued, "has been obvious to all; but on what particular occasion constructed, was a matter of doubt."

Although Jeffersonian common sense has since prevailed and we now attribute the creation of the Great Serpent Mound—"discovered" in 1848 by American archaeologists Ephraim Squier and Edwin Davis—to its Native American builders, the meaning of the serpent remains as murky as ever. As with every

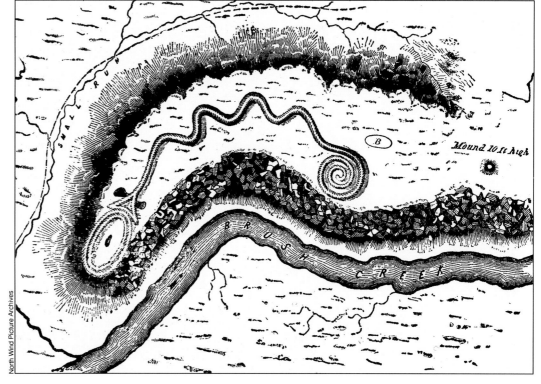

The Adena Indians, who built the Great Serpent Mound sometime after 1000 B.C., inspired and influenced many other tribes who subsequently created animal-shaped effigy mounds throughout the Midwest and even the South. Witness today the earthwork of the prolific Hopewells in such sites as the Mound City Group National Monument in Ohio (inset) as well as Georgia's Rock Eagle Indian Mound (right).

the shape of pyramids, while many others have been molded into discernibly animate forms such as eagles, elks, foxes, bears, buffaloes, and of course, snakes. A few have even been shaped like men and women. Needless to say, each mound has a story or two that purports to explain its origins and significance, but no prehistoric mound is as majestic, as meaningful, or as mysterious as the Great Serpent Mound in Bratton Township, Ohio.

Stretching above a steep cliff along the eastern side of Ohio Brush Creek in Adams County, at close range it looks like nothing more than a long, undulating mound of earth. From a distance or from the air, this rock, clay, soil, and sod sculpture appears to be a dead-on reproduction of a serpent, coiling and uncoiling for nearly a quarter of a mile (0.4km).

This 1,254-foot (381m) -long Great Serpent Mound, as we now call it, is believed to have been built between the reign of King Solomon and the pinnacle of the Mayan empire—probably sometime after 1000 B.C.—by a people we now refer to as the Adena.

Not much is known about the origins of the Adena. Most of what we've learned about this agrarian people—who were among the first to grow maize on this continent—comes from the thousands of burial mounds they built. Archaeologists have discovered, for example, seven-foot skeletons, which we can only assume were once seven-foot Adena.

Inside the burial mounds, the Adena built rectangular tombs for the corpses and filled them with some of the deceased's worldly possessions, including stone pipes shaped like humans or animals, tablets made of stone that were adorned with abstract or animal designs, and copper objects hammered into various inanimate and animate shapes.

Most of what we know about the Adena has come from the thousands of burial mounds they built. Inside the mounds were rectangular tombs filled with some of the deceased's worldly possessions and bones stained red with ocher. Remarkably, some of these skeletons measured seven feet (2.1m) tall.

Archaeologists who excavated these Adena mounds found that many of the bones were stained with red ocher, the result of a ritual that can be dated back to around 2400 B.C. according to similar discoveries made at Red Lake in New York State. They were also able to discern from these remains that the Adena had unusually high foreheads, which were probably intentionally induced by binding the infants' skulls at birth. This practice also had its roots elsewhere; similar prehistoric skull shapes have been located in Central America and Mexico.

No one knows precisely what the serpent represented to the Adena or what its great, earthen manifestation was supposed to tell us. In many early cultures, trees, serpents, and fire were common symbols of worship. Few creatures, however, inspired the extraordinary awe, fear, and superstition in prehistoric (and even contemporary) people as did (and does) the serpent. The Egyptians worshiped the serpent under various guises, as did the Assyrians, Indians, and Samothracians—the practice is called ophiolatry—and it's likely that the Adenas did, too. Mostly, the serpent served as a phallic symbol to these cultures, often as some totem of fertility.

The serpent is also connected to water—which, of course, has fertilizing powers. Some have speculated that the Great Serpent Mound unites the life-giving properties of earth and water in a union that transcends the death of the flesh.

There has even been considerable discussion concerning various parts of the serpent's anatomy, most specifically the mouth. At least that is the most commonly held explanation for the triangular-shaped portion of raised earth—presumably the serpent's head—that is opened wide, apparently clutching something in his jaws. Most of the questions raised have to do with this large oval above the serpent's mouth. Some have suggested that the oval represents an egg about to be devoured by the serpent, while others believe that it depicts a view into the wide-open jaws of the serpent itself. And then there are those ascribing to the former opinion who take the egg-shape theory to the heights of reproductive symbolism—too convoluted to detail—involving egg, sperm, and coition.

The Great Serpent Mound, which is up to twenty feet (6m) wide in some places, was painstakingly built—obviously—to last. It was originally outlined upon a smooth surface along the ridge of a hill. Near the west end of the oval, where the serpent is slithering up the steeper portions of the hill, the base seems to have been made with stones, most likely to prevent the structure from being washed away by heavy rains. In some spots, this bottom layer has decomposed into gray clay. On top was spread from one to six feet (0.3 to 1.8m) of yellow clay from the region, which filled in all the irregularities of the rock. Then a five-inch (13cm) to almost two-foot (0.6m) -thick layer of dark soil was added, and over this was placed a layer of sod. Throughout the body of the serpentine figure were a series of small holes in the clay, which varied from a few inches to more than one foot deep and from two to seven feet in diameter. Their position and the fact that they contained animal bones or ashes indicates that they were placed there intentionally. For what specific purpose, we do not know.

The Adena no doubt influenced many of the neighboring cultures. Animal-shaped effigy mounds abound in southern Wisconsin, northwestern Illinois, eastern Iowa, and even Georgia, in addition to those found in the Ohio Valley. Many of these mounds feature animals—mammals, reptiles, birds—whose feet (assuming they have feet) point downhill. Most are about one hundred feet (30m) long and are built low to the ground along a ridge.

From about 300 B.C. to about A.D. 600, a second group of mound builders, who probably overlapped with the Adenas, left an equally prolific output of mounds in the area but seemingly fewer mysteries. We call these builders the Hopewell Indians, which is a moniker bestowed posthumously—courtesy of a farmer, Mordecai Hopewell, who permitted a dig on his property near Chillicothe, Ohio, in 1891.

The Hopewell mound building spanned the Ohio and Illinois river valleys—curiously, nearly all the burial mounds were built near rivers or tributary

Unlike their mound-building brethren who stocked grave sites with extraordinary works of sculpture and pottery, the people of the South Appalachian Mississippi culture created their great temple mounds to worship gods. They were, however, ancient masters of their crafts, which included this pair of male-female ancestor god figures.

streams—with much more complex and larger earthworks than those of the Adena. Some of their customs, however, were similar. For example, they also made elaborate soapstone pipes in the shapes of animals and humans.

Again, we learn most of what we know about the Hopewell people from their grave sites. Archaeologists who've excavated their mounds discovered artifacts and objects that presumably had come from all over what we now call North America: obsidian knives from Wyoming, sharks' teeth from the Gulf of Mexico, silver from Ontario, hammered-copper ornaments from Lake Superior, mica from the Carolina Smoky Mountains, and in extraordinary abundance, strings of freshwater pearls. It seems very likely that the Hopewell Indians were a group of active traders—and perhaps even industrious hikers—who were willing to go that extra mile for a good deal.

© Courtesy Georgia Dept of Natural Resources

In his book *Mound Builders of Ancient America*, Robert Silverberg wrote that "there is a stunning vigor about Ohio Hopewell, a flamboyant fondness for excess that manifests itself not only in the intricate geometrical enclosures and the massive mounds but in these gaudy displays of conspicuous consumption." He was referring, of course, to the practice of having corpses laden from "head to feet in pearls, [weighed] down in many pounds of copper, [surrounded] with masterpieces of sculpture and pottery, and then [buried] under tons of earth . . ."

The "enclosures" that Silverberg refers to were wooden mortuary houses, usually without roofs, that looked like large stockades. Inside these enclosures, the Hopewell cremated most of their dead after removing the flesh from their bones. Only the ruling elite were left with their corpses intact. And while it seems that all of the Hopewell dead were given some goods to service them in the next life, it was the privileged few—maybe the upper one-quarter of the tribe—who were lavishly decked out in the excessive manner previously described.

The symbols and shapes found on many of these burial treasures appear similar to those used by the Adena—in particular, the serpent—but the Hopewell employed many new designs of their own, notably sun disks and swastikas.

The apex of the Hopewell era was probably around 100 B.C. to A.D. 200, more than one thousand years before Columbus made it over to the "new" world. Their influence was great at this time, spreading into Indiana, Michigan, Iowa, Wisconsin, and Missouri. But they eventually went the way of the Adena, into the mist of history, leaving to this New World a magnificent legacy.

Temple Mounds

INFLUENCED MORE BY CENTRAL AMERICA THAN THE burial mounds of the Adenas and Hopewell are the earthworks of the mighty Mississippians. They were the builders of North America's great temple mounds—rarely used for graves, but mostly as sites for worshiping their gods. Much like the pyramids of the Aztec and Mayan peoples, these earthen structures featured stairways and ramps topped by temples (in the case of the Mississippian structures, these were made of wood).

The Mississippian culture began around A.D. 700 and probably continued through the fourteenth century. The city of Cahokia, located across the Mississippi River from St. Louis in what is now Illinois, housed a population of perhaps ten thousand in a large complex of rectangular plazas. Surrounding the plaza were flat-topped mounds, some of which were temples and many of which were houses for the priests and other city officials. Every small village in the outlying "suburbs" of Cahokia had its own temple mound, stretching the city's reach much like Teotihuacan (in Mexico) did on a grander scale when it became the center of the Mayan empire (see page 108).

Of the approximately one hundred mounds in and around Cahokia, the most mammoth was Monk's Mound; located in the heart of the city, this one-thousand-foot (304m) -long, seven-hundred-foot (213m) -wide, and one-hundred-foot (30m) -high earthwork was (and is) the largest in the world.

By the time Columbus and the ensuing slew of European explorers clambered onto the shores of the New World in earnest, the Mississippian culture was all but gone, with the temple mounds its most visible and most lasting landmarks.

The Marching Bear Group, built by the Woodland Indians in what is now Iowa, is the second-largest group of effigy mounds to be found in the United States.

© Courtesy of Effigy Mounds National Monument;Photo by Allan Zarling

EASTER ISLAND

The Riddle of the South Pacific

Easter Island's forbidding, foreboding stone statues (previous page and opposite) have outlasted whatever mysterious, industrious civilization that created them. Carved out of Rano Raraku, an extinct volcano on the eastern end of the island, the heads were lowered down the mountain using ropes and hauled off on sleds to platforms.

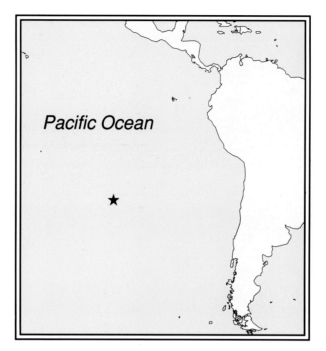

Pacific Ocean

Thousands of miles from anywhere, lost in the vastness of the South Pacific, sits a silent stone riddle called Easter Island.

The great sculpted heads of this strange place have awed and puzzled men since Easter Sunday in 1722, when a Dutch ship accidentally "discovered" a speck of land nearly 2,500 miles (4,000km) off the coasts of Peru and Chile. To this day, the eerie, mystical attraction that the island holds is no doubt due in great part to the brooding and foreboding (and forbidding) mien of these outsize stone heads. If they were softer, more cartoonish, or even cuddly figures, it is likely there would be no Easter Island mystique.

But these statues are anything but warm or inviting, and certainly no one has ever described them as cuddly. They sit with their backs to the ocean, showing apparent disdain and defiance of the outside world. Who built them? Where are their descendants now? When were they built and why? What do they represent? If only these stone heads could talk.

Even for statues, they appear particularly mute. Looking inward, always inward, they don't seem eager to share their mysteries. Nor do they seem to care much for their history or for the people who created them. They seem to say: Whoever was once here, whatever civilization was ingenious enough to create such mighty monuments, they're not here now. We outlasted them all. We are still here.

There is much disagreement regarding the identity of the original Easter Islanders, the people who built these huge, silent creatures. There are those who say that they were inhabitants of the "lost world" of Lemuria, a race of giants, and that the heads were simply life-size representations of them. Some claim that the heads were the images of extraterrestrials who visited the island in prehistoric times, while still others believe that the heads were merely *built* by the extraterrestrials.

Serious archaeologists believe that the original inhabitants were the Lapita, a race of potters and sailors who made their way across the South Pacific from Fiji to New Guinea around 1000 B.C. and, riding the southeast trade winds, eventually landed their canoes on this isolated island sometime during the third or fourth century A.D.

Pointing to Polynesians as the likely ancestors of Easter Island, other scientists note the cultural similarities; they say that South America—the other likely site for settlers—is too "distant," in cultural as well as geographical terms.

The renowned Norwegian archaeologist, Thor Heyerdahl, believes that the island was settled by people from the east, pointing to the comparatively light skins of the islanders found by the Europeans who arrived here in the 1700s. To prove his point, Heyerdahl arranged a dramatic demonstration. In 1947, he set sail from the coast of Peru on a balsa raft called *Kon-Tiki*—a craft he built that was similar to those used by many South American people of the era.

Heyerdahl's journey was a success. He reached Easter Island in his tiny, fragile craft, proving, at the least, that the voyage was possible. To some, that's all he proved.

But recent computer studies indicate that it is virtually impossible for a boat to drift to Easter Island. Therefore, it is more than possible that some people—perhaps from what is now Peru or Chile—set sail deliberately on an expedition or an emigration.

Whoever the original Easter Islanders were, someone was inhabiting the island before A.D. 400—the earliest period that has been carbon-dated. And during this early period, roughly A.D. 400 to 1100 (scientists have ascribed names and dates to the three stages of Easter Island development), a large number of ceremonial terraces were built, most of which were oriented toward the rising sun. During this early era, some small statues were built—made of different types of stone—but none on a grand scale.

The middle period (1100–1680) islanders were a remarkable people, and although we still know little about them, they left a remarkable legacy. The 600 heads found on the island—some weighing up to fifty tons (46t) and some standing thirty-two feet (9.7m) high—are believed to be a small fraction of the original total built during this period. Where did the others

© Anna E. Zuckerman/Envision

The distinctive topknots, created from reddish rock mined from another volcano on the island, were attached as the giants lay prone at the base of the volcano before being carted away.

go? Some were destroyed by man and/or nature; some were stolen; and some, including a colossal sixty-eight-foot (21m) head, still lie in the amazing natural quarries from which the islanders obtained the stone used to manufacture their great sculptures.

The way in which the giant statues were built is one of the few things about Easter Island that we do know. Ancient quarries have been found at the extinct volcano of Rano Raraku on the eastern end of the island. Here, islanders carved out the tuff of the volcanoes, chipping away with their stone tools, until a sort of prehistoric Mount Rushmore appeared—giant heads attached to the volcano only by a spine of rock. The statues were then lowered with ropes down the side of the mountain. The final touches—which included the red topknot created from the reddish rock mined from another volcano on the island—were applied as the giants lay prone at the base of the volcano.

The big problem, of course, was how to transport the statues from their quarry to their *ahu*—the raised stone platforms, many of which had been converted from the earlier ceremonial terraces, on which the heads were to be erected. The ancient Easter Islanders wasted little time reinventing the wheel; in fact, they never got around to inventing it in the first place. Instead of carts or wagons, it is believed that the huge, heavy stone sculptured heads were hauled on sleds and then raised onto their ahu via a stone ramp or a system of levers. Once the heads were supported on their platforms, the eyes were inlaid "open" with coral whites and the irises were made from the same red volcanic tuff as was used for the topknots.

The arduousness of this labor cannot be underestimated. What could it have been like for these people to work without metal tools, without even the most

basic wheeled vehicles? It's been estimated that it would have taken thirty men a year just to carve out *one* of these statues, and that ninety men, working for at least five months, would have been required to transport a single head from the quarry to the ahu, and add to that, of course, the time it would have taken just to erect it.

For a society with barely a few thousand inhabitants, it was one of the most prodigious investments of time and labor in (barely) recorded history. Yet, the motive behind such a massive undertaking—a mind-boggling construction project—remains as obscure as the identity of the builders.

When famed British explorer Captain James Cook visited the island in the eighteenth century, he was told by the natives that each of the statues had a name. As a result, some contend that the heads were an ambitious form of ancestor worship, likely reserved for Easter Island "royalty"; that each statue representing an actual native chief or king (which the islanders called an *ariki*) was erected to overlook the lands and fields ruled by that particular monarch. Since the ahu was acknowledged to be a funeral platform, magnificently decorated and arranged with precisely carved stones, this would seem to be a plausible explanation. Still, how do we explain the similar look of each statue—the elongated heads, the long ears, the blank, expressionless faces?

Clearly, the spiritual beliefs behind the statues must have been powerful ones. Fresh water and vegetation were so scarce on Easter Island that early European settlers could stay only briefly. Indeed, part of Heyerdahl's theory is that the early sailors who came in their *Kon-Tiki*–like rafts were stranded on the barren, sixteen-mile (26km) -long island because the material that they needed to repair their balsa boats was unavailable.

The early Easter Islanders had no pottery—a fact which would argue against South American origins, since the clay work of the Andean peoples was so highly developed—and they survived by fishing and basic farming; their crops included yams, bananas, and sugarcane. Their subsistence way of life—with such minimal resources and an apparently primitive culture—makes their stone achievements even more amazing. How could these unsophisticated natives construct stone heads the size of modern two-story buildings? And how could so many of them remain intact—and even standing—after hundreds and hundreds of years?

What could have driven them to such avid displays of devotion to their kings, ancestors, or gods? Reverence certainly. Perhaps it was fear or appeasement of some great power, or maybe just the hope that something or someone would deliver them from their hardships and isolation.

This isolation helps illuminate the singular nature and mysterious aura surrounding both the island and the slew of monuments. It may also provide an expla-

Evidence of unfinished business remains at the Rano Raraku quarry as a reminder of the great seventeenth-century war that decimated the island's inhabitants.

The Bird Cult of Easter Island

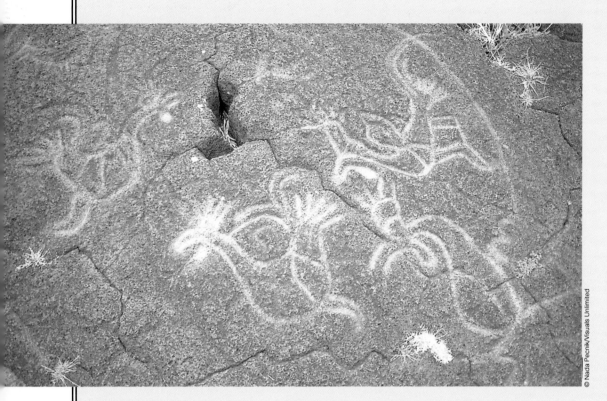

© Nada Pecnik/Visuals Unlimited

day, however, no one has been able to crack the code of *Rongo rongo*.)

It was believed that this was the site of an annual ritual of great significance. It was at Orongo that the members of prominent families would gather and send their servants swimming to the small, nearby island of Motu Nui. The objective was to gather the first eggs laid by the migratory sooty terns. The master of the servant who found the first egg was honored for the entire year.

The rise of the cult of Makemake and the Orongo rituals does not necessarily explain the motives of the statue builders. But it does demonstrate again the importance of the spiritual life of these islanders—a power that apparently drove them to create such an incredible legacy, a power that ultimately destroyed them.

Found throughout the island are petroglyphs, such as those of chickens (above and right), whereas the written devotions to the bird-god Makemake—in a script called Rongo rongo—remain undecipherable to modern code breakers.

WHAT FORM OF WORSHIP COULD HAVE MOTIVATED THE islanders to focus the energies of an entire society on such a mammoth construction task? Some believe it might have been the bird cult, a "religion" that apparently flourished on Easter Island around 1500.

The clues to the mystery of the bird cult lie in the village of Orongo, which is near the crater of the volcano Rano Kau on the southwestern tip of the island. This ceremonial village of fifty stone houses seems to have been the center of the cult of the bird god Makemake. The houses in the villages were adorned with carvings of bird-headed men, some of whom were depicted carrying eggs, as well as strange writing. (In the nineteenth century, a set of wooden tablets was uncovered, filled with an unknown script that was called *Rongo rongo*. To this

© Richard Harrington/FPG International

nation for why the statues brood. When the Dutch and English explorers reached the island in the 1700s—during the so-called late period (1680–1868)—they found few houses. What they found instead was a race of people so frightened and impoverished that they were literally living underground. The great stone-making culture of Easter Island had been reduced to a dismal life spent dwelling in caves and a few simple thatch-roofed huts.

As the Europeans pieced together the story, apparently around 1600, a great war disrupted a long period of relative prosperity. In a way, one could say that the conflict was precipitated by the statues themselves.

The limited timber supply on the island was used in the statue-building effort—mainly for the sleds to transport the heads and the levers to erect them. As the timber dwindled, the soil deteriorated. The result was famine, and according to both legend and some scientific discoveries (numerous spearheads were found from this period), a war between two factions known as the "Long Ears" and the "Short Ears" began. The series of conflicts may have lasted for decades. It was said that as the famine took hold, each side resorted to the cannibalization of captive women and children. Needless to say, the statue building ceased, and whatever spiritual meanings the great heads might have held at one time were likely lost amid the carnage and despair.

By the eighteenth century, when the European explorers reached the island, the culture was in deep decline. No doubt the "civilized" powers expedited the process. In 1862, Peruvian slave ships carted off any able-bodied islanders to work in the mines. Most of them died en route, while others died of disease in Peru. The few survivors who returned to the island

© Wolfgang Hille/Leo De Wys Inc.

spread smallpox and leprosy. By 1877, the population of Easter Island was 110—about one human being for every six statues. In 1888, Chile annexed the island—and presumably brought better food and medical care to the decimated people.

Is there any wonder why these giant heads brood so profoundly and inarticulately? No words can express the horror of what they have seen—the disintegration, destruction, and death.

The silent statues of Easter Island avert their sad eyes and turn their backs on the rest of the world. Remnants of a civilization that will forever be lost, they also stand as sentinels of hope.

They are still here.

While some experts contend that these great heads were a form of ancestor worship, most likely honoring local chiefs or kings, there has not yet been a plausible explanation for the similar look of each statue.

GLASTONBURY

King Arthur's Reputed Resting Place

Steeped in legend and lore concerning the Holy Grail and the great landscaped zodiac, Glastonbury is also the rumored resting place of King Arthur.

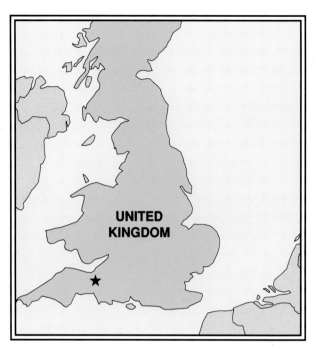

UNITED KINGDOM

Lording over the flat plains of the English countryside like an aging but still regal king, Glastonbury Tor announces itself as an unmistakable landmark for one of England's most legendary places.

There is the legend of the Holy Grail, the chalice purportedly used by Jesus at the Last Supper; there is the legend of the zodiac, rumored to be written in the landscape; and then there is one of the greatest legends of them all, that of King Arthur, who is said to be buried somewhere beneath the ruins of Glastonbury Abbey.

In ancient times, when Christians first settled here, Glastonbury was virtually an island, with the seas saturating most of the lowlands between Mendip Hills and Quantock Hills in what is now called Somerset County.

Glastonbury's history prior to the eighth century is rather vague. Around A.D. 700, a monastery was built, most likely by King Ine; in the tenth century, it became a Benedictine house. The main abbey church was built in the thirteenth and fourteenth centuries, and much of the remains are on view today.

The legend and lore of Glastonbury is much less vague. For example, Joseph of Arimathea, the rich man who wrapped up the body of Jesus and carried it to his tomb, later came to Glastonbury by boat (and eventually founded a church there). Arriving at Wearyall Hill, he climbed out of the boat with the aid of his wooden staff, which as this enriched legend has it, then took root and grew into the Glastonbury Thorn, which still flowers on Christian holidays.

There is no richer or more multifaceted legend than the one (though there are at least several permutations) that has sprung up around the great King Arthur.

Believe it or not, some skeptics—much like the ones who reject Shakespeare as the sole producer of Shakespearean works—dispute the nobleman's very existence.

The twelfth-century Benedictine monk Geoffrey of Monmouth is often credited with being the first person to fully chronicle—some would say embellish—the story of King Arthur in his *Historia Regum Britanniae* (History of the Kings of Britain). Geoffrey cited as his primary source a "most ancient book in the British tongue" presented to him by the archdeacon of Oxford. That work, however, has never been located.

Earlier sources confirm that a valiant leader named Arthur lived around the sixth century. One of the foremost of these sources was Nennius, a ninth-century cleric, who in his *Historia Britonum* (which some say was not an original work) wrote of Arthur's battles: "Arthur fought against the Saxons alongside the kings of the Britons, but he himself was a leader in the battles. The first battle was at the mouth of the river which is called Glein . . . The twelfth was on Mount Badon, in which—on that day—there fell in one onslaught of Arthur's nine hundred and sixty men; and none slew them but he alone, and in all his battles he remained victor." Nennius indicated the year was A.D. 518.

The tenth-century *Annales Cambriae*, the ancient Welsh annals, contained a passage that also "confirmed" Arthur's life (and death). It cited A.D. 539 as the year when the "battle of Camlan in which Arthur and Medraut [Arthur's nephew] were slain; and there was death in England and Ireland . . ." The question we have today is where Camlan (or Camlann, as it is sometimes spelled) might be. Speculation has placed the site in locations from north Wales to Cornwall to Somerset.

Geoffrey wrote that from Camlan, or wherever, Arthur was carried to the Isle of Avalon, his final resting place, also known as the Otherworld, the Delightful Plain, the Land of Promise, and so on. Through the ages, there has been continued speculation of legendary proportions that from this perfect world Arthur might still one day return.

The remains of the great Arthur are possibly interred somewhere beneath the ruins of Glastonbury Abbey in Somerset County.

There is no richer legend in written lore than that of King Arthur (below) and his valorous Knights of the Round Table (right).

In Malory's renowned *Le Morte d'Arthur*, published in 1485, the final battle between Arthur and Modred (as Malory referred to the traitorous nephew) took place on a field near Salisbury. According to Malory, virtually all of the Knights of the Round Table met their demise there, and Arthur, after killing Modred, proceeded to fall "in a swoon to the earth and there he swooned many times."

In Malory's version, Sir Lucan and Sir Bedivere, two of the surviving Knights of the Round Table, assisted their mortally wounded king to a small chapel by the sea. There Arthur asked Bedivere to cast Excalibur into the sea, whereupon "there came an arm and a hand above the water and caught it, and so shook it thrice, and then vanished away the hand with the sword into the water."

Before heading out into a waiting boat, in which sat three lovely fairies (some say they were Arthur's sister and two ladies-in-waiting), Arthur turned to his faithful knight Bedivere and said, "Comfort thyself, and do all thou mayest, for in me is no trust to trust in. For I must into the vale of Avilion to heal me of my grievous wound. And if thou hear never more of me, pray for my soul."

And into the mist went Arthur, presumably for Avalon, which some students of ancient lore believed was an island similar to the place of perfection in Irish mythology.

The traditional legendary belief holds that Avalon was Glastonbury and that the most likely location for this unlikely event was at the mere, now drained dry, at Pomparles Bridge near Glastonbury. There has also been some indication that the bodies, if not the spirits, of both Arthur and Guinevere were buried in the abbey there.

King Henry II, the great-grandson of William the Conqueror, accepted this as gospel—even more so when he was informed by a Welsh bard of the precise location of Arthur's grave: between two pillars just south of the Old Church at Glastonbury.

Henry then ordered the abbot of Glastonbury to investigate, but on May 5, 1184, before any excavation could be done, a fire destroyed all of Glastonbury's church buildings, including the abbey, the old church, and the newly built Norman church. The king immediately dispatched his steward, Ralph Fitz-Stephen, to oversee the reconstruction of the Glastonbury shrines. Unfortunately, poor Henry died in 1189, one year before the discovery of the controversial leaden cross.

It all began when an old abbey monk died. The monk had requested a burial site between the two pillars in the old church, the very site that the bard had cited as Arthur's grave. Church and state officials cordoned off the area and began digging. Approximately seven feet (2.1m) down, workers reputedly struck a stone slab. Underneath the slab, they pulled out a heavy leaden cross with the inscription: HIC IACET SEPULTUS INCLYTUS REX ARTURUS IN INSULA AVALLONIA ("Here lies buried the renowned king Arthur, in the isle of Avalon").

Imagine the excitement attendant to such a discovery. Here was proof positive that the renowned Arthur, England's most well-known legendary king, did indeed exist; and moreover, Avalon—the isle of light and heavenly peace—might indeed also exist.

The discoveries did not end there. Even some of the monks joined the frenzied shovelfest, and at about sixteen feet (4.8m) down, something large, solid, and wooden was uncovered: a hollowed oak log, often used by ancient Celts as a coffin. And indeed, bones were soon extracted from the log—first a human shinbone, obviously from an individual of extraordinary height, and then a human skull, crushed on the left side, perhaps from a blow received in battle.

Did not Geoffrey of Monmouth describe such a lofty height (eight feet [2.4m]) for the slain (as a result of a blow to his left ear) Arthur?

On May 5, 1184, a fire destroyed all of Glastonbury's church buildings, including the abbey, the old church, and the Norman church. Remains of the Glastonbury Abbey, built in the thirteenth and fourteenth centuries, can still be seen today.

© Topham/The Image Works

Visitors to the picturesque
town of Glastonbury can
view the Tor in the
distance.

More bones were unearthed, some of which were obviously from another individual, a much smaller, more delicate person with yellow hair. Guinevere? That's what it purportedly read on the side of the coffin.

If one's skepticism is sorely tested here, there could be good reason. The Glastonbury monks were in dire need of funds to complete their restoration efforts. Might not a few shrewd men be capable of staging such a hoax, fueled all the more by the fact that only a few disinterested observers ever saw the bones? (Think about it: Wouldn't the exhibition have provided large sums of money for the new monastery?)

Still, reputable sources seem to have verified various aspects of this discovery. The antiquary John Leland apparently viewed the inscribed cross in Glastonbury during the reign of Henry VIII. And William Camden, respected headmaster and author of the guidebook *Britannia*, provided a drawing of the lead cross in the book's sixth edition in 1607. Modern scholars who have studied Camden's rendering, however, are not in agreement concerning the authenticity of the lettering.

While some experts have identified the lettering of the cross's inscription as belonging to the sixth century—Arthur's purported era—a well-respected authority, Professor Leslie Alcock of Glasgow University, author of the book *Arthur's Britain*, maintained that "the inscription is not in the fifth or sixth century lettering, but several centuries later. In my mind, if the cross as illustrated ever existed, then it was a Tudor tourist trophy."

In 1962, British archaeologist Dr. Ralegh Radford confirmed that Arthur's purported *original* grave site at the Glastonbury ruins had most likely been an ancient burial place—indicated partly by the disarranged stones he found there—but he had no way of telling to whom the grave had once belonged. While the monks supposedly "reburied" the remains of Arthur and Guinevere, or whoever it was in those two coffins in 1190, their bones were dug up again—in the presence of King Edward I, in 1278—and again reinterred in a black marble tomb before the high altar of the (then) refurbished Glastonbury Abbey. Those remains might have remained there if it were not for the vandalism and desecration that occurred over the years, most likely during Henry VIII's so-called "Dissolution of the Monasteries."

Today, Arthur's original grave is unmarked but lies just a few yards away from the south door of the twelfth-century Lady Chapel.

Glastonbury was also the reputed site of another incident involving King Arthur. It was there that his queen, Guinevere, was kidnapped and held by King Melwas of Somerset—possibly in the King's stronghold on top of the 500-foot (152m) Glastonbury Tor. Before a bloody battle could ensue, the abbot intervened and a settlement was negotiated.

The Tor today is encircled by a winding path of terraces that rewards visitors to the summit with an intimate view of the ruins of an ancient church tower—the remains of a church built by the ancient monks and dedicated to St. Michael the Archangel. The tower's weather-worn frontage still bears the visible carvings of some very bizarre—some might say pagan—tableaux, such as the devil "weighing" a human soul against the world, a woman milking a cow, and a pelican plucking its breast. The meaning of such curious carvings remains unexplained.

The meaning of the Tor's role in the so-called Glastonbury Zodiac may be more defined, if no more

Thomas Malory, "Knights" Writer

BY THE EIGHTH CENTURY A.D., THE TALES OF ARTHUR HAD been celebrated in several sources and were already a major component of British folklore. But it wasn't until the so-called Christian writers began to chronicle the king's exploits that the Arthurian legend took on, well, legendary, significance.

This trend probably began with the supposedly historical tome *History of the Kings of Britain*, by Geoffrey of Monmouth, who even in his own time was appreciated more for his imagination than his scholarship. Then there came the anonymous *Death of Arthur*, written about A.D. 1245, as well as the works of Chrétien de Troye, the most famous of which was probably *Lancelot*. All of these works, among others, were utilized by Thomas Malory in his epic cycle, *Le Morte d'Arthur* (The Death of Arthur), published by Caxton in 1485.

Malory's saga is probably the definitive work on the king, his wife, and his knightly court. It is a story filled with romance, chivalry, derring-do, courage, and death. Yet, ironically, the teller of these legendary tales spent twenty years of his life in prison for crimes that one may charitably call "unchivalric."

Born of a good family, a soldier in the Hundred Years' War, and knighted for bravery, Malory even served in Parliament in 1445. Then, inexplicably—certainly we have no definitive explanation for his behavior—he embarked on a life of rape, poaching, extortion, and jail-breaking. It was during a stint in prison that Malory wrote this "noble and joyous book" (as described by his publisher), his only known work.

The text contained eight parts, or tales, including "King Uthur and the Coming of Arthur," "King Arthur's War with Rome," "Lancelot," "Gareth," "Tristam," "Sangreal" (Holy Grail), "Knight of the Cart" (also about Lancelot), and finally, "Le Morte d'Arthur."

Le Morte d'Arthur begins with the birth of Arthur and ends, of course, with his death as well as the dismantling of the fabled Round Table. In between, he was the ideal of medieval chivalry. Malory made unforgettable characters of Galahad, Lancelot, and Gawain, not to mention Guinevere and Arthur. It is an emotionally charged work, as well as a deeply melancholy one. In many ways, it is one of the most seminal in the English language, and it served as the model for a number of great English poets—including Tennyson, who in the nineteenth century reworked Malory's material in *Le Morte d'Arthur* (later revised as *The Passing of Arthur*) and *Idylls of the King*.

Malory died in Newgate prison in 1471.

Thomas Malory's seminal fifteenth-century work, Le Morte d'Arthur (The Death of Arthur), was published posthumously.

North Wind Picture Archive

explainable: for reasons best known to the ancients of astrological bent, Glastonbury Tor purportedly was used as part of the Aquarius figure in the Glastonbury Zodiac, which was laid out in a ten-mile (16km) -diameter circle landscaped into the Somerset environs.

At the foot of the craggy Tor is an old well, filled as much with the all too well-defined meaning of legend as with its renowned blood-red waters. Science has an explanation for its discolored spring waters: it is tinted red from iron oxide. But what to make of the noises coming from the well's spring water that sound so much like that of a beating heart?

Some call it Blood Spring, but most refer to it as Chalice Well, because it was here that the invaluable and magical Holy Grail was reportedly hidden. The famous chalice, believed to have been used by Jesus at the Last Supper, was thought to have been brought by Joseph of Arimathea over to England when he fled his homeland. Because of its mystical, miraculous powers, the great Grail was sought in vain by virtually every ancient adventurer with a taste for fortune, salvation, and the meaning of life—including several of King Arthur's knights. They, however, like everyone else before and after, never found it.

What we find in Glastonbury today is more mystery than fact. It may be Avalon, and it may be the site of the Holy Grail, but it is certainly much like it was when the twelfth-century chronicler William of Malmesbury called it "a heavenly sanctuary on earth."

The doorway to the Chapel Crypt (above) leads to the Blood Spring, so called because of its iron oxide–tinted waters; another name is the Chalice Well, given to the site because the mystical, unattainable Holy Grail (above left) was supposedly hidden here.

PALENQUE

A Mayan Architectural Jewel

Bleached white by centuries of tropical sun, the limestone temples and pyramids of Palenque (previous page) are located in what is now the state of Chiapas in southern Mexico.

There are few sights more unsettling than the ruins of a once-great city. One feels both loss and bewilderment when confronted with the remains of an illustrious civilization buried under the inexorable growth of creepers and vines, a vivid sign of the passing of time. The ruins of Meso-America are famous not only for their beauty and intricacy, but also for the ghostly echoes of the tens of thousands of their inhabitants—all of whom vanished at the end of a single millennium. Descendants of this highly developed race still inhabit the land where their forefathers founded kingdoms, and the old tongue continues to be spoken in a variety of forms, but the Mayas of antiquity simply disappeared, leaving only traces of ruined cities.

Bleached white by centuries of tropical sun, the limestone temples and pyramids of Palenque sit nestled in the rain-forested mountains of southern Mexico, in the state of Chiapas. Of all the sites so far uncovered in this wide region, Palenque is arguably the most magnificent. Visitors frequently say that it is jewellike, and indeed the cluster of well-proportioned, wonderfully carved structures in the classic Mayan style are singular in their dazzling craftsmanship and beauty.

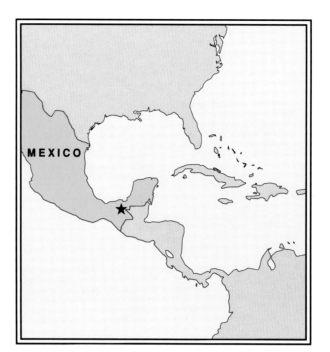

Palenque is also unique for the relatively short period of time in which it flourished. Its golden age lasted a mere 200 years—from A.D. 600 to 800—beginning with the rule of Pacal, whose name means "shield" in English. The explosion of art and architecture was carried on by King Pacal's son, Chan-Bahlum, or "snake-jaguar," who, not to be outdone by his prolific father, commissioned an amazing number of stone works that glorified his family as descendants of the gods.

In the past three decades, great breakthroughs have been made in the decoding of Mayan hieroglyphs by investigators who have exposed much of this once-shadowy world. And only now can we begin to appreciate the depth and complexity of Mayan society, a culture that many feel rivaled those of ancient Egypt, Greece, and Rome in its richness and vigor. Like those earlier cultures, the Mayan civilization took root and grew to prominence in a verdant area that allowed the necessary shift toward agricultural cultivation.

Mayan culture was born about 200 B.C. in the region that stretches from the lower half of Mexico to the middle of Central America. At the height of its glory, this civilization could claim more than fifty autonomous city-states, each ruled by a dynastic family. Millions of people, ranging from nobility to peasant farmer stock, were governed by these lords of the land whose power was god-given and absolute.

Cities of palaces, temples, and open plazas grew, supporting huge urban populations and clearing the way for the development of art, written language, and ritual. Sadly, only the durable art remains; as is the case with other lost civilizations, none of the Mayas' written material has survived, having long since decayed or met with destruction at the hands of the conquistadors. Some records were left, however: set into stone, the carvings of the Mayans are proof that their brief history was indeed glorious.

The art and architecture of Palenque are some of the most unusual and instructive in the world. The grandest structure is that of the Temple of Inscriptions, named for the hieroglyphs discovered inside. Built by Pacal against the side of a mountain, this pyramid is topped by the temple that houses the inscriptions. As was the case with the Khmer god-kings in southeast Asia (see page 36), Pacal's architectural achievement became his tomb after his death, and in 1946, archaeologists were amazed to uncover his skeleton.

This finding was indeed a rare switch from the common Mayan practice of cremation; Pacal's body had been carefully interred in an ornate stone sarcophagus. The upper temple building had apparently func-

The Temple of Inscriptions, named for the intricate hieroglyphs found inside, was built on a mountainside by the great King Pacal.

Cracking the Mayan Code

REMARKABLE AS IT MAY SEEM, THE GRAND MAYAN RUINS of Palenque lay undiscovered in the thickly jungled Yucatán lowlands until 1785, when the Spanish explorer Antonio del Rio happened upon them. They were popularized in the nineteenth century by the collected notes and drawings of John Lloyd Stephens and Frederick Catherwood, travelers who first brought the Mayan culture to light. It wasn't until the 1960s, however, that contemporary detectives were able to make sense of the ancient Mayan language carved in perpetuity into limestone stelae and temple walls.

The most recent breakthroughs in decoding the Mayan tongue have been made by a team of scholars led by Linda Schele and David Freidel, who have been studying the ruins of these ancient civilizations since the early 1970s. As a painter and an archaeologist, respectively, their backgrounds helped them find the repetitions of image patterns and make sense of a hieroglyphic structure that is an amalgam of several different methods. The Mayan carvings were apparently an adjunct to a highly developed written language that was lost to decomposition and fires set by Spanish invaders because it utilized paper like our own. Schele and Freidel's systematic investigation of Mayan ruins and the stone carvings with which they are littered has led to a major enlightenment in the understanding of this culture. They have deciphered the names of kings, their ascendancies, and many other historical elements that were ritually preserved in rock. It seems as though the Mayans intended these documentary reliefs to be carried down through the ages so that human beings would always know of these rulers and their great deeds.

Comprised of symbols and phonetics, the hieroglyphs, which were thought for centuries to be merely decorative, are mostly of the rebus type. For instance, a carved

Comprised of symbols and phonetics, these hieroglyphic carvings (right and above right) are the only "written" record of Mayan culture; they were seemingly used as an adjunct to a highly developed language put down only on paper—lost forever due to decomposition and the fires set by Spanish invaders. Resembling sophisticated cartoons, each hieroglyphic inscription generally represented an incident in the life of a king.

eye literally represents the word *I*. The language of ancient Egypt is similar in nature and comparable in its spare phraseology. It has been pointed out that the crude materials the Mayans used—hard stone and basic cutting tools—also cut down on verbosity. Even so, known Mayan hieroglyphs number almost five hundred, a hefty collection by any standard. The stories these pictographs tell exploded many myths surrounding the Mayans; many scholars had previously labeled them a strictly peaceable and pastoral people. Instead, a portrait emerged of a society for whom life was dictated by blood rituals and sacrifices, for whom war—as ordered by the demigod kings—was a frequent occurrence.

Mayan hieroglyphic inscriptions generally represented an incident in the life of a king with a notation of time, place, personage, and event carved along the border of

© Haroldo & Flavia de Faria Castro/FPG International

the depiction. Resembling sophisticated cartoons, these historical artworks have provided a wealth of information about the royalty who were this hemisphere's Tutankhamen and Jayavarman. The mystery these hieroglyphs do not reveal, however, is why the culture so suddenly ceased to exist. What happened to the millions of citizens who left their cities to crumble into dust, who vanished almost three hundred years before the Spanish slashed their way through Mexico and Guatemala? So far, no stone carvings have been found to explain this phenomena.

David Freidel, the archaeologist whose breakthrough work with Linda Schele has led to many remarkable discoveries about the Mayans, sums up the lasting enigma of this lost world: "We cannot open the Mayan portals to the otherworld with excavation alone, no matter how careful and how extensive, for the portals are places in the mind and in the heart. We, as pilgrims from another time and reality, must approach the ruined entrances to the past with humility and attention to what the Maya, ancient and modern, can teach us through their words as well as their deeds."

tioned as a kind of historical repository for Pacal, who had artisans create three giant limestone stelae that have since been found to include a long list of Mayan kings' names. A depiction of these very same kings also appears on Pacal's casket as a literal representation of the ancestral lineage that connected all the Mayan kings. These kings' effigies are marvelously represented as the fruit of a spiritual garden; their royal heads appear to be growing out of the soft earth.

Pacal's queen and his son Chan-Bahlum's queen also appear on the stones, sometimes engaging in a graphic bloodletting ceremony: members of the royal family drawing a rope through a wound in their tongues and directing the flow of blood into a vessel designed to catch the stream. Other images recount great battles fought between the kingdom of Palenque and its neighbors; depictions of severed heads represent power because highborn victims were often sacrificed to the gods in this manner. These carved histories point out clearly that there was little or no separation of political might and religious practice. One unconditionally supported the other.

Instead of the usual Mayan practice of cremation, King Pacal's body was painstakingly interred in a stone sarcophagus in the Temple of Inscriptions (left).

Dominating the Palenque skyline is the four-story observatory tower rising out of Pacal's palace.

© Nefsky/Art Resource: Mayan Stucco Mask, 800 A.D. Mexico, Private Collection

King Pacal's reign was long and energetic. He ascended to the throne at the tender age of twelve and remained there, seemingly unchallenged, for almost sixty years, after which his son assumed the mantle. It appears that father and son were also highly competitive. The rock carvings illustrate a kind of heroic one-upmanship that continued even beyond death. There is evidence that some of the carvings in the tomb of Pacal had been altered after his demise to include representations of Chan-Bahlum taking part in important events. It may have been that Chan-Bahlum's hold on his constituency had become weaker at some point around A.D. 800, and it became more important for the "snake-jaguar" to elevate his importance in the eyes of the gods.

The Palenque complex is dominated by the palace, which sits at the center of the building plan. Its architectural features are quite extraordinary, especially its four-story observatory tower and advanced structural engineering. Along with carved stucco walls and friezes, the palace features apartments, arched galleries, courtyards decorated with elaborate bas-relief sculptures, and a plumbing plan that allowed for fresh water and even a steam bath. Four more temples, built mainly by Chan-Bahlum, were added to Palenque, including the Temple of the Sun, which is dominated by a spectacular wall frieze.

The most extraordinary aspect of Palenque, however, were the Mayas who dwelled there. After all, they were the architects of these masterpieces; they were the builders whose talent gave meaning to the mute rock. What they lacked in technology—the Mayans' tools were very crude and even though they knew about the wheel, they didn't put it to use—they made up for in societal organization and industriousness.

This stucco mask was made around A.D. 800, during the latter stages of the reign of Pacal's son, Chan-Bahlum, who presided over the final days of the Mayan golden age.

Located at the center the Palenque complex, the palace featured carved stucco walls and friezes, arched galleries, and courtyards decorated with bas-relief sculptures.

The driving force behind this busy civilization was worship, which for the Maya was completely inseparable from life itself.

The Mayan view of religion featured strong ties to the supernatural and was rooted in the belief that everything is cyclical in nature. Some of their ways of veneration may seem bizarre by modern standards, but they make sense when examined as a literal extension of their beliefs. The practice of ritual bloodletting, performed frequently and often depicted on the stones of Palenque, was meant to foster and maintain life. Physical existence for the Maya could not prevail without spiritual devotion, and the kings, as direct descendants of the gods of the sun and underworld, served as the divine priests joining those two worlds. Their intercessions between this world and the other maintained the balance and unity that ensured survival, health, and wealth.

Bloodletting ceremonies were undertaken on the temple pyramids of Palenque to encourage the materialization of otherworld beings into animate and inanimate objects. Blood was the sacred red river that brought together heaven, the middle world of earth, and the underworld to guarantee the vitality of the whole. The tongue and male genitalia provided the holiest sources of blood for these ceremonies, motivating greater communion with the beings responsible for protecting the repetitive cycles of history.

Interestingly, the Mayas—who physically resembled the North American Pueblo Indians—shared, or perhaps passed on, this holistic belief system that all things, from rocks to trees to insects, possessed a life force. Their religion also involved directions and colors that corresponded to north, south, east, and west, much like the Native American practice of today.

Still, the dutiful Mayan propitiation of the gods did not spare Palenque from the mysterious cataclysm that wiped out its entire population, leaving the forgotten city to be consumed by the hungry and unrelenting jungle. There are no answers to the mystery of this vast disappearance, only hints of what might reasonably have taken place. Excavations of a wide area of Palenque have turned up remains that point to the possibility of a plaguelike sickness or widespread malnutrition as the fundamental cause. After one thousand years of a thriving and successful culture, how could hunger and illness have defeated the Mayas of Palenque?

Perhaps the kings themselves were to blame, battling each other to the point where the fields lay trampled and fallow. Perhaps it was a massive turn away from the faith that had sustained them after their confidence in the god-kings had been shaken. Perhaps it was an unknown event even more catastrophic.

© J.G. Sidaner/Art Resource

© D. Donne Bryant/FPG International

Although Palenque's population was ultimately destroyed by a mysterious cataclysm, its magnificent Mayan buildings—such as the Group of the Cross, which was built around A.D. 750—remain a silent testament to the greatness of the culture.

Whatever the reasons, it seems hard to believe that within 160 years after the glorious zenith of Palenque, the city had become victim to wandering tribesmen squatting in the decomposing temple ruins. Evidence has been found of the small trinkets and tools these squatters left there, marking their nomadic presence. Bodies have also been discovered buried beneath the collapsed rubble; with nobody there to help, the occasional drifter became just another interesting archaeological find, one more strange clue in the downfall of a great and highly productive nation.

Descendants of these Mayan kings still dwell in the Yucatán and other areas. They continue to speak languages that derive from the two original Mayan tongues and often worship in much the same way—except for the sacrificial rites and offerings of blood. What remains lost to archaeologists was also lost to them. Only now are modern Mayas—with help from researchers—beginning to learn the language of the hieroglyphs. They, too, are beginning to win back the history and the legends of heroes that was stolen from them by misfortune and time.

Bibliography

Arundel, John, and Robert Cooke. "Unburying Mystery of Pyramid Builders." *New York Newsday*, April 2, 1991.

Broyles, William, Jr. "Uncovering A History of Heroes." *U.S. News & World Report*, June 2, 1986.

Ciochon, Russell L. "Jungle Monuments of Angkor." *Natural History*, January 1990.

Cotterell, Arthur. *The Macmillan Illustrated Encyclopedia of Myths & Legends*. New York: Macmillan, 1989.

Davidson, Robyn. "Rock Dreams." *Mother Jones*, October 1989.

Haining, Peter. *Ancient Mysteries*. Great Britain: Hutchinson of Australia, 1977.

Hawkins, Gerald S., and John B. White. *Stonehenge Decoded*. Garden City, N.Y.: Doubleday, 1965.

Houk, Walter. "The Best of Ancient Mexico." *Travel/Holiday*, September 1982.

Huth, Tom. "The Great Empty." *Condé Nast Traveler*, September 1990.

Mitchell, John G. "The Serpent." *Audubon*, November 1986.

Nickell, Joe, et al, comps. "The Big Picture." *Scientific American*, June 1983.

Pochan, Andre. *The Mysteries of the Great Pyramids*. New York: Avon, 1978.

Randell, E. O. *The Serpent Mound, Adams County, Ohio*. Columbus, Ohio: Ohio State Archaeological and Historical Society, 1905.

"Reports & Comment: 'The Longest Day.'" *The Atlantic*, June 1987.

Riley, Frank, and Elfriede Riley. "Pacal's Reign." Los Angeles, January 1990.

Roberts, David. "Tantalizing to Scholars and Tourists, Carnac's Megaliths Remain an Enigma." *Smithsonian*, September 1989.

Sugaraman, Aaron. "Revealed." *Condé Nast Traveler*, December 1990.

Warner, Roger. "After Centuries of Neglect, Angkor's Temples Need More Than a Facelift." *Smithsonian*, May 1990.

West, Richard. "It's Ancient History." *Travel & Leisure*, September 1989.

Westwood, Jennifer, ed. *The Atlas of Mysterious Places*. New York: Weidenfeld & Nicholson, 1987.

Wilson, Ian. *Undiscovered*. New York: William Morrow, 1987.

Index

Aborigines, 48, 49, 50, 51, 52, 53, 53
Adena Indians, 84, 86, 87, 88
Alcock, Leslie, 104
Alice Springs (Australia), 49
Altar stone, 31
Amazon jungle, 58
American Notes (Dickens), 82
Ancestor worship, 94, 97
Andes Mountains, 56
Angkor Thom, 40
Angkor Wat, 37, 38, 39, 39, 41, 42, 43, 43, 44, 44, 45, 45
Angles, 32
Apsaras, 43, 43
Arthur, King, 100, 101, 102, 102
Arthur's Britain (Alcock), 104
Atahualpa, 61
Aubrey, John, 29, 31, 34
Aubrey holes, 29, 31
Australia, 48–53
Avalon, 101, 102
Ayers, Sir Henry, 49
Ayers Rock, 47, 48, 49, 49, 50, 50, 51, 51, 52, 53, 53
    color, 48, 49
    sounds, 49
Aymara Indians, 17, 17
Aztecs, 61

Bakong, 41
Baphuon, 41
Bayon, the, 40, 40, 41, 42
Beltane Fire, 35
Bingham, Hiram, 56, 61
Birds, 12, 13, 13, 16, 96
Blood Spring, 107, 107
Bluestones, 29, 30
Bronze Age, 30
Burial grounds, 16, 22, 25, 31, 71, 83, 86, 87, 88
Burn pits, 15

Cambodia, 38–45
Camden, William, 104
Camlan, 101

Capac, Manco, 56
Capac, Huayna, 61
Carbon dating, 25
Carnac, 20, 21, 21, 23, 24, 25
Carpet snake people, 50, 51
Catherwood, Frederick, 112
Celts, 31, 34, 35, 35, 71, 103
Cerne Abbas, 25, 65, 66, 67, 67, 68, 70, 70, 71
Chalice Well, 107, 107
Chan-Bahlum, 110, 113, 115, 115
Chapel Crypt, 107
Chephren, King, 76
Chile, 61
Colombia, 61
Commodus, Emperor, 67
Cook, James, 94
Cortes, Hernan, 61
Cromlechs, 21, 22, 22, 28, 30, 32
Cruz-Moquen, 25
Cuzco, 56

Davis, Edwin, 83
del Rio, Antonio, 112
de Troye, Chrétien, 106
Devatas, 43, 43
de Vega, Garcilaso, 63
Dickens, Charles, 82
Dingoes, 49, 53
Dolmens, 21, 22, 22, 23, 23, 25
Donnelly, Ignatius, 82
Dragon Hill, 71
Dreamtime, the, 50, 51, 53
Druids, 20, 25, 31, 32, 34, 35, 35

Earthworks, 28, 82–89
Easter Island, 91, 92, 93, 93, 94, 95, 95, 96, 97, 97
Eclipses, 25, 31
Edward I (King of England), 104
Effigy
    figures, 12
    mounds, 89
Egypt, 74–79
England, 28–35, 66–71, 100–107
Entasis, 30

Equinoxes, 35
Excalibur, 102
Extraterrestrials, 14, 15, 25

Fairy Stone, the, 20, 25
Fertility
    images, 51, 66
    rites, 25, 68
    symbols, 67, 87
Flight, 15
France, 20–25
Freidel, David, 112, 113

Galahad, 106
Gallic Wars (Julius Caesar), 35
Gawain, 106
Geoffrey of Monmouth, 100, 103, 106
Giza, 73, 74, 75, 75, 76, 77, 78, 78
Glastonbury, 100, 101, 101, 102, 103, 103, 104, 107
Gosse, William, 49
Great Pyramid of Cheops, the, 74, 75, 77
Great Serpent Mound, the, 81, 82, 83, 83, 84, 87
Great Sphinx, the, 74, 76, 76
Group of the Cross, the, 117
Guatemala, 61
Guinevere, 104, 106

Hadingham, Evan, 25
Hawass, Zahi, 77
Hawkins, Gerald, 14, 31, 35
Helestone, 28, 30, 31
Helith, 67
Henry II (King of England), 103
Henry VIII (King of England), 104
Hercules, 67, 68
Heyerdahl, Thor, 93
Hieroglyphs, 111, 112, 112
History of Dorset (Hutchins), 68
Holy Grail, the, 100, 107

Hopewell Indians, 87, 88
Hopewell, Mordecai, 87
Hutchins, John, 68

Idylls of the King (Tennyson), 106
Imhotep, 75, 79
Incas, 12, 58, 59, 61
Indians
    Adena, 84, 86, 87, 88
    Aymara, 17, 17
    Aztec, 61
    Hopewell, 87, 88
    Inca, 12, 58, 59, 61
    Mayan, 43, 61, 110, 111, 112, 113, 115, 116
    Nasca, 12, 13, 14, 15, 16, 17
Indravarman I (Khmer king), 39, 41
Inti, 59
Intihuatana, 58, 59
Iron Age, 68, 71
Irrigation, 39, 41

Jayavarman II (Khmer king), 38, 39
Jayavarman VII (Khmer king), 40, 41, 45
Jefferson, Thomas, 82, 83
Joseph of Arimathea, 100, 107
Jutes, 32

Ka-Hief, 74
Ka-M-Ankh, 74
Kangaroos, 49, 53
Kercado, 20
Kerlescan, 23
Kermario, 23
Khafre-Ankh, 74
Khensu, 79
Khmers, 38, 40
Khufu, 74, 77
Knights of the Round Table, 102, 102, 106
Kon-Tiki (Heyerdahl), 93
Kosok, Paul, 13, 14
Kurapunyi, 53

Lake Titicaca, 17, 17
Lancelot, 106
Laos, 38
Lapita, 92
Le Grand Menhir Brisé, 20, 25
Leland, John, 104
Le Menec, 21, 23
Le Morte d'Arthur (Malory), 102, 106
Lemuria, 92
Le Petit Menec, 23
Lethbridge, T.C., 32
Lizards, 12
Llamas, 12
Long Man of Wilmington, 69, 70, 70, 71
Looting, 44
Loti, Pierre, 41

Machu Picchu, 17, 55, 55, 56, 56, 57, 57, 58, 59, 59, 60, 62, 62
Mahabarata, 43
Makemake, 96
Malory, Thomas, 102, 106
Marching Bear Group, 89
Mayans, 43, 61, 110, 111, 112, 113, 115, 116
May Day rites, 68
Megalith Builders, 28
Megaliths, 19, 20, 21, 22, 22, 23, 24, 25
Menes, 74
Menhir, 21, 22, 22
Mercury, 68, 71
Mexico, 61, 110–117
Mitchell, John, 82
Modred, 102
Mohammed, 68, 71
Monkeys, 12
Monk's Mound, 89
Monoliths, 32, 48, 91, 93, 97
Mound Builders of Ancient America (Silverberg), 88
Mound City Group National Monument, 84
Mount Badon, 101
Mount Meru, 43
Mulga-seed Clan, 53

Nasca, 12, 13, 14, 15, 16, 17
  shapes drawn by, 11, 13
Necropolis, 74

Nefer, 74
Nennius, 101
Nen-Sedjer-Ka, 74
Neruda, Pablo, 62
Nickell, Joe, 15
Northern Territory (Australia), 49

Observatories, 14, 20, 25, 31, 34, 38, 44, 58
Ophiolatry, 87
Osiris, 79
Otherworld, 101

Pacal, (King of Palenque), 110, 111, 113, 115
Palenque, 38, 43, 109, 110, 111, 111, 114, 115, 115, 116, 116, 117, 117
Peru, 12–17, 56
Petroglyphs, 96
Pizzaro, Francisco, 61, 61
Pottery, 12, 15, 16, 16, 30, 67
Prasat Kuk Bangro, 44
Preah Khan, 40, 41
Preah Ko, 41

Radford, Ralegh, 104
Radiocarbon dating, 20
Ramayana, 43
Reiche, Maria, 14, 15
Reliefs
  carved, 43
  sculptural, 40
  shallow, 43
Religion
  Buddhist, 43, 44, 45
  Celtic, 35
  Hindu, 38, 39, 40
Religious icons, 16
Renfrew, Colin, 31
Rock Eagle Indian Mound, 84

Sacrifices
  animal, 16, 17
  human, 34, 35, 35, 59
St. George, 71
St. Paul, 68, 71
Saqqara, 74, 79, 79
Sarsen blocks, 30, 32
Saxons, 28, 32, 101

Schele, Linda, 112, 113
Scotland, 32
Seshem Nefer I, 74
Set, 79
Shiva, 39
Silverberg, Robert, 88
Snakes, 12
Solstices, 25, 28, 30, 44
South America, 56
Spalling, 53
Spiders, 12
Spohrer, Jim, 15
Squier, Ephraim, 83
Stephens, John Lloyd, 112
Stiles, Ezra, 82
Stonehenge, 22, 27, 28, 29, 29, 30, 30, 31, 33, 34, 34, 35
  alignment in, 28
  design of, 30
  ground plan of, 29, 31
Stukeley, William, 31
Sun worship, 30, 58
Suryavarman I (Khmer king), 41
Suryavarman II (Khmer king), 39, 41, 43, 44

Ta Prohm, 40
Tello, Julio, 13
Temple mounds, 89, 89
Temple of Inscriptions, 111, 111, 113
Temple of the Sun, 115
Tennyson, Alfred Lord, 106
Thailand, 38
Thom, Alexander, 25
Thomas, H. H., 29
Tiwaz, 68
Totemic cairns, 16
Trendle, 68
Trilithons, 30, 32
Tumbes, 61
Tutankhamen, 74, 77

Uffington White Horse, 70, 70, 71
Uluru, 50, 51, 53
Uluru National Park, 49, 52
Urubamba River, 56

Valley of Kings, 74
Vandalism, 45, 104
Vietnam, 38
Vilcabamba, 56, 57, 61
Viracocha, 59
"Virgins of the Sun," 58
Vishnu, 38
von Däniken, Erich, 14

Wales, 32
Wallabies, 49
Westbury White Horse, 70, 70, 71, 71
William of Malmesbury, 107
Wise, Francis, 71

Yasovarman I (Khmer king), 41

Zodiac, 104, 107
Zoser, King, 79
Zoser's Pyramid, 74, 79